FLEECED - HOW I GOT FLOCKED BY LOVE & THE LAW

And how to knit yourself a better future

Cinoma Bronhill
Tobia G. (illustrations by)

ISBN-13: 9798878476508

Cover design by: Tobia G.
Produced in Canada
Printed in the United States of America

www.barkinginthewilderness.com

*For Dad, who fought alongside me and told
me I had to write this book*

"An unjust law is no law at all"

ST AUGUSTINE OF HIPPO

CONTENTS

Title Page

Copyright

Dedication

Epigraph

INTRODUCTION   3

PART ONE: 8
STILL WOOLY

Chapter 1: Culled Ewe   9

Chapter 2: Fairy Sheep & Lamb's Tales   18

Chapter 3: What's that in Yer Haggis?   28

Chapter 4: Are Ewe Being Petty?   36

Chapter 5: Aesop's Tails & Merino Wolves   45

Chapter 6: Lamb Stew   58

Chapter 7: Unravelled   68

PART TWO: 76
INTO THE CHUTE

Chapter 8: Terms of a Shearing   77

Chapter 9: Sheep-Dipped by Contract   84

Chapter 10: Partially Flocked   90

Chapter 11: Udderly Flocked   101

Chapter 12: But Still Kicking   113

PART THREE: KNIT A DIFFERENT FUTURE 122

Chapter 13: Two Lambs Don't Always Make a Ewe 123

Chapter 14: Mind Your Fences 129

Chapter 15: Green(yer) Pastures 139

Chapter 16: Is Dick Milking Ewe? 148

Chapter 17: Other Chops of Lamb 155

Chapter 18: Don't Get Unravelled 161

Chapter 19: Ram v. Ewe 174

Chapter 20: Write Your Cohab for Ewe 191

Conclusion: Darn Your Wool 206

APPENDICES 220

Appendix 1: My Legal Journey 221

Appendix 2: Quick Links to Family Law in Your Jurisdiction 229

Appendix 3: The Cohab I Wish I Had Written 231

END NOTES & BIBLIOGRAPHY 251

Acknowledgements 259

About The Author 261

Fleeced

How I got Flocked by Love & the Law

and knit yourself a better future

by Cinoma Bronhill (my pseudonym)

Illustrated by Tobia G. & the Author

INTRODUCTION

I can't knit a stitch but my sister raises sheep, or at least she used to. She fed them, cared for them, named them, sheared them, made sweaters and scarves from their wool, helped them have their babies, and sometimes had them for supper. She stopped doing it because it bothered her how the sheep would slump their big woolly bodies against her, the one who once cared for them so well, passively accepting their fate, whether it was to be fed, sheared, or slaughtered.

This is exactly what we do when we expect the law to do right by us. To be fair and dispense proper justice. And when we partner up and cohabitate with someone, maybe someone we don't know as well as we think we do, yet we expect that true love will prevail. Yeah, that sheep? That was me.

Why didn't I read a book like this? I often ask myself this. Why didn't I, after some dust had settled on the divorce papers of my twenty-year marriage but before the hurts had healed, when I found myself "out there" looking for love again? Why didn't I, after I met Mr. Wonderful and thought I'd met my soulmate, listen to the churnings inside me (no, not *those* churnings, those are the ones that get us into trouble in the first place!) when he said he wanted to move in with me? Why didn't I at least find out what was at stake? Well, years later, poorer, still wounded, wondering why the winters are so chilly, I know why. And I want to share it with you so you don't suffer my fate.

For one thing, while there are a lot of great books providing legal advice on family law, and megatons of books on relationships, there's not very many on how emotional trauma, lack of boundaries, and relationship dysfunction translate into a fleecing in a family law court, and how a rocking cohab agreement might have saved the day. I wish so badly that someone had written a book like this. But even if they had, would I have actually *read* it, before I said yes when Mr. Wonderful asked if he could move in? Sure, there were warning signs, but we were in love! And love conquers all kinds of dysfunction, right? Just ask the fans of Hugh Grant films.

Guilty as charged. I didn't read a book like this because I believed in those fairy tales, the rosy hues of rom-coms, meet cutes, soulmates, and all that stuff, so I didn't pay attention, until it was too late. Meanwhile some of you are entering into, or coming out of, true partnerships, where everything you built, and the life you had, was created together. If one of you stayed home to take care of the kids, or who sacrificed career and success so your partner could soar, for those who did the airport pickups and soccer drop-offs. Family law is there to protect you, and it should.

But does it?

Now, some of you might say I'm bitter: a woman scorned. Some might say I believe in financial security more than true love. Or that I'm so angry that I can't let it go, that I'm a sore loser and this is just a swipe at the ex who got away with it. Others will think that I'm arrogant for writing this when I'm not a family lawyer. Maybe some of that is true, but I worked and consulted with thirteen lawyers, and several therapists, in my battle with my ex, in an effort to save my house, my future, and my sanity. And now I'm here to tell you what the lawyers won't.

First, I'll tell you how I got involved with someone who ended up reneging on every single promise he ever made to me, and yet still managed to get family law on his side. My story is a cautionary tale: about the post-divorce dating world, how first family trauma can infiltrate our choices in love, how our deeply buried wounds prevent us from standing up for ourselves and what we believe is fair, *and* about how family law really works. It was a hellishly painful, not to mention expensive, eye-opener for me about the costs of getting involved with someone before wounds are healed and our values are properly defined. I hope you are reading this before you get into the same boat I hopped into, but either way, it's gonna sting.

After that, the book is about what really happens during a break-up followed by a family law action, and why this is especially painful if you have moved in with someone who you thought was Mr./Ms. Wonderful who turns out to be a Mr./Ms. Wrong. If, like me, you don't have a bullet-proof cohabitation agreement, you might as well learn what it feels like to walk that plank, and what not to do so you don't end up sinking and feeding some fishes. Another hellishly painful and expensive eye-popper, not only on how family *actually* works, but how it really plays out both in and outside of the courtroom. It's not *Drop Dead Diva*, that's for sure. Yet, against all odds, I chose to fight. And how well did that go? That's part two of the book.

As we go along this journey, I'll tell you what I learned

about the law, and what I wish I had done differently. This heartbreak at the hands of a Mr./Ms. Wrong and a shearing at the hands of a blind Lady Justice could have been prevented, and I will tell you how in Part Three. What I'm going to tell you will not only keep you out of court, it could even *save* your relationship. Or at least help you decide if this relationship is one you really want to have.

My hope, with this book, is that you benefit from the battle I had to fight, that by reading this you learn from my mistakes as well my victories, as you contemplate a new relationship and a co-mingling of both emotions and of assets. Especially those of us who went into that co-mingling after some money was made and hearts were broken, maybe later in life, and met someone (probably online), who had all the answers to all our sorrows. This book is for those of us building a life with another person for the first time, but also for those with assets we gained on our own, who met someone while we were trying to rebuild and recreate—our lives, hearts, and self-esteem - after being cast aside by someone we loved. No matter how many times you have thrown your heart, your hopes, and your future into the ring, this book is for you—empaths, optimists, hopeful and hopeless romantics - but most of all for the wounded, for those of us looking for a love that will heal. Calling all fauna in the headlights...

I wrote this for you...

PART ONE:
STILL WOOLY

CHAPTER 1:
CULLED EWE

One look into those sleepy, sad blue eyes and I was a goner. Even now, years later, I'm not 100% sure why. "He's not even that good-looking!" my friends would cry. In hindsight I can see what they mean. More an aging Alfred (as in E. Neuman) than a Ryan (Reynolds, Gosling, Seacrest, your pick), with greying wiry hair and sun-damaged skin. Plus, I think I weighed more than he did. Even worse, he had bad shoes! An obvious thrift-store purchase, which is a fine and sustainable thing to do, but these looked like something you'd find in the back of Elton John's closet disguised with shoe polish. My guard was up.

Okay you got me. I was a bit of a princess. Okay, okay, more than a bit. My ex-husband is Italian and his footwear—sneakers, sandals, boots—has always been sublime. So decent shoes became one of my standards, along with clean fingernails. Both were a must. But this time, for some reason, they didn't matter. I was smitten, besotted, bedazzled, absorbed, incredibly randy, and temporarily insane. All for an unemployed dude who looked like the mascot from Mad Magazine? With bad shoes? What were you thinking? you may ask. Well, he smelled really good and knew where all the buttons were (given how many women he'd had, it would be weird if he didn't) and he ticked all the common-interest boxes. But other than that, at the time at least, I had no idea. I just had to have this skinny, poorly shod, generously endowed (I'm talking about the ears!) guy in my life and in my bed. It wasn't until I stood in the middle of the toxic smoking-debris field of our seven-year relationship that it started to dawn on me why I had been so Svengali'd. It had absolutely nothing to do with him and everything to do with me. But at this point I was a long, looooong, way from figuring that out. All I knew when I first kissed him was that if I didn't keep this man in my life, I would die.

[#]

We all want love. So badly that some of us are willing to risk the farm to take a chance on child-hood dreams and the rom-com spin of sunsets and never-ending bliss. The two questions I ask myself, after going through the most painful experience of my life, is: 1) how did I get here, and 2) what could I have done to prevent this from happening to me? How we become vulnerable to financial loss, and in some cases you could even call it predation, through those who claim to love us, is one part of the story. How family law facilitates this, is the other.

A cull ewe is what those in the sheep biz call a female sheep that is no longer useful. It means she is no longer suitable for breeding, usually due to her age, and will be discarded from the herd and sold for meat. That's how I felt after my divorce...

Mistake No. 1 (of many) was that I started looking for that fantasy, that rom-com love, long before I had even begun to recover from the breakup of a twenty-year marriage. A few months after my husband's father died, he announced he needed to have children and left me for a woman he worked with who was a decade and a half younger than me and, unlike me, still able to have his kids. In an eye-blink, my idyllic princess life was over and I had become a middle-aged cliché.

Ok, in reality, relationships never really end in an eye-blink. People say, "Oh, I never saw it coming!" They saw it, all right. They just didn't want to look. I certainly didn't, and now here I was jobless—after a cancer scare, I gave up a lucrative career as an engineer to pursue a lifelong dream of becoming a writer. I was penniless—feeling guilty over giving up said lucrative career, I gave every dime I made as a writer to the accounts my husband controlled. I was homeless, with a dying dog and a schizophrenic cat—because my husband sold our house. But worse than any of that, the one person, the only person, who I thought would always love me, no matter what, suddenly no longer did. Then along comes this other man who tells me that the reason he never settled down, why he had so many women, why he wandered the earth, usually penniless, was that he was desperately seeking, questing, yearning, searching for...

Me.

And those few easily said words were a warm soothing balm to my wounds: the big, raw, and ragged gaping holes in my emotional psyche I didn't even know I had. Plus, I'm competitive and Mr. Wonderful subtly goaded me: "C'mon on down, ladies; step right up, girls. Because you're the next contestant on Who's the Best Woman for Meee?..."

Oooo-ooo, pick me, pick me! I am! I am!

I was doomed, is what I was.

When I first split from my husband, he told me that a) I had brought this on myself by being both a brat and too old to bear the children he now desperately wanted, and b) that I was going to get a piece of the house once we sold it, no spousal support, and no part of his pension. I believed him, on both counts, and started desperately looking for a job and an apartment that would take someone with no income and three animals. In Vancouver. Good luck! But on the advice of a friend, I spoke to a lawyer and started learning about family law. I don't think my then-husband appreciated what it meant when he decided to leave his wife of twenty-odd years who didn't have a job and being on the wrong side of forty, was unlikely to get one, or at least a job that would maintain her in the lifestyle to which she had become accustomed. He thought he could sell the house, give me my share, and say sayonara. Especially since I'd been such a spoilt brat these past few years, chasing my screenwriter dreams with trips to Cannes and LA and refusing to give up my prized showjumper to boot. Surely, the law wouldn't let someone like me claim spousal support. Surely, this ne'er do well couldn't be entitled to a portion of his pension. Could she?

Think again.

The introduction of "no-fault" divorce, initiated in the US in 1969 by then Governor of California Ronald Regan,[1] was ground breaker because for the first time in recent history, anyone could divorce just because they felt like it. No preconditions like adultery, abuse, larceny or whether or not the marriage had been consummated. If you wanted out, you were out, with a share of the familial assets, no (or at least very few) questions asked. Canada followed suit with the revised *Divorce Act* of 1986, which enabled division of assets and spousal support more or less evenly, regardless of who had contributed to what asset and who had done what to whom.

"For the first time in Canada, formal legal equality of support rights and obligations was established between men and women, and the right to spousal support went from a fault concept to an economic one based on needs and ability to pay.... During the 1970s and 1980s, many provinces and territories enacted legislation that virtually eliminated the offence concept as the

foundation of spousal support rights and obligations. In addition, following the precedent established by the federal Divorce Act of 1968, the right to spousal support on marriage breakdown in the absence of divorce became no longer confined to wives under provincial and territorial legislation; a financially dependent spouse of either sex might look to his or her marital partner for financial support."[2]

The financial outcome of the dissolution of my marriage shocked everyone, including me. My ex-husband's family, with whom I had once been very close, refused to take my calls. My own mother, already really pissed at me for, as she put it, taking advantage of a nice man and ruining my marriage, was aghast at what the lawyers said I could take. "I didn't take spousal support or your father's pension when he left me" she said to me. "But maybe that's because I had a decent job. Which you did, once, before you quit."

I'm paraphrasing but you get the gist. Jobless, homeless, and scared, I took what family law said I was entitled to. Every cent. But while I was now in a position where I wasn't going to end up on the street and didn't have to sell my showjumper for steak tartare, it came wrapped in a crushing sense of guilt. I felt guilty. Really, really guilty. Even more guilty than when I was in the marriage. Come to think of it, my husband was really good at making me feel guilty. And inadequate. A lot like my Mom did... which is maybe why I left home so young, or felt the need to escape into the fantasy of film during my marriage. My own mother thought my ex was the bees' knees. So did his family. Ipso facto, despite being the one getting ditched, I was the asshole. I'm the deadbeat who took too much of the house and a chunk of my ex's pension. This is the narrative of myself that I took into the next chapter of my life.

Whether I should have felt all that guilt is another story, but it was a vulnerability that led me to make some choices I would later regret. First family issues, guilt, poor self-image, are just some of the things that can leave us vulnerable, questing for someone who promises to love in the way that our parents, kids, friends, and ex-spouses never could. Sometimes we find those people, sometimes we find wolves in merino sweaters. Knowing what the law says they are entitled to is something I think we all need to learn before we let any of them move in with us.

In Canada, the *Constitution Act, 1867* gives the federal government the ability to regulate marriage and divorce under its *Divorce Act*[3]. When a couple separates, they have certain entitlements under the federal act, such as child custody and spousal support, as well as under their provincial or territorial Family Law Act (*FLA*), such as property and pension division. The provinces are also responsible for applying the laws, such as ensuring spousal support, if awarded, is paid. Marriage and divorce in the US, however, fall completely under the jurisdiction of state governments, which means the laws of the state, or states, where you and your spouse live, apply to everything.

Despite the regional differences, general trends are similar across both countries, whether you're getting married, becoming common-law, or splitting up.

Meanwhile, in efforts to keep up with rapid societal change and political climates, the law is ever-changing, and it is possible to get caught between changing laws and new acts. I know because it happened to me.

In British Columbia, where I live, the provincial *Family Law Act* governs property and asset division. Right around the time I was getting together with Mr. Wonderful — you know what, let's just call him Dick, Dick Chancer, for reasons that will become obvious — BC repealed its *Family Relations Act* and enacted the *Family Law Act* in early 2013, which instantly gave cohabitants the same rights to property and spousal support as marital spouses. Lawyer No.1,[4] who was drafting our initial (and flawed) cohab agreement, wasn't sure how this was all going to pan out and did the best she could in an unstable situation. The cohab was flawed because it presumed that Dick would keep his side of the bargain, and I was too busy being in love (and probably gaslighted, but more on that later) to register the implications but can't help but wonder if Dick had been doing his research.

I'll tell you how I ended up with a Dick in the next chapter. For now, think of the law like the medical system: while we use the services and tools it provides us, such as making appointments and taking advice from our doctors, we need to take responsibility for our own health and what happens to our bodies. Same with the law and our financial, and emotional, future. In my case, when he decided he wanted to be with someone else, my ex-husband should have learned the legal consequences of splitting up a twenty-year marriage from a spouse at her lowest earning potential, instead of making *me* out to be a jerk for accepting what the law said I was owed.

Here's what I learned about the Law: it has evolved to protect the lower-earning spouse, regardless of the circumstances

Here's what I learned about Love: Guilt can cull ewe (sorry, couldn't help that)

What you can do: Learn the basics of family law in your jurisdiction before moving in with anyone.

CHAPTER 2: FAIRY SHEEP & LAMB'S TALES

Beware of the fairy-tale romance, the promise of everything you've ever dreamed of, of people who open our closed-up boxes and fill the holes in our souls. If it feels too good to be true, it usually is.

If you're completely smitten, can't keep your hands and your minds off them, sacrificing friends and passions to be with them and forgetting to feed the cat, it's a strong signal you're heading into a toxic relationship. But I was years away from realizing that. All I knew was, after one terrible dating experience after another, that I was in love. Truly, madly, deeply in love, like I'd never been before, not realizing this passion was a product of biology, history, and too many movies. If you had told me that, a few years later I would be poring over self-help videos and online journals on personality disorders and mental health conditions, trying to figure out what made Dick tick, desperate to understand what he was doing to me and why, I would have called you crazy.

[#]

If you accept evolutionary theory (I realize not everyone does) then you know that our species has been around for less than a nanosecond of Earth time, and it's only been a few hundred years, since the Industrial Revolution, that our best-before date started to improve and we stopped dying toothless and worn out at age forty-five. Now at forty-five, we're just getting started. While a huge portion of the population is still dying way too young a few of us get to live way longer in relative luxury. With gym-toned muscles, surgically-improved chins, perky boobs, chemically-enhanced appendages, money in the bank, and the kids out of school, we sip oxygenated water while swiping through endless online profiles, wondering when we're suddenly going to see him/her, the shining face, wreathed in champagne and rainbows, the signal of hope and our sparkly future... The One.

And sometimes there will be more than one "One". Because we don't just live one lifetime anymore; we get to live two or three lives, if we're lucky enough to be born in a first world country and some nasty hidden gene or a drunk driver doesn't take us out. People pivot and change as they live those lives and what we want in our twenties changes when we're in our forties—and we may even get another do-over in our sixties or seventies. Take my step-mom, who just took up line dancing a year shy of eighty. And who was Mr./Ms. Perfect decades ago suddenly no longer fits the bill. That certainly happened to me. My husband was in his forties when he realized he no longer wanted the free-spirited West Coast hippie he'd left the East Coast for. His mortality and familial duty suddenly bore down upon him and he needed a different life, not to mention someone who had a set of bursting ovaries.

I was changing too. After getting a taste of death, I suddenly felt trapped in the frame my husband had built for me. He wanted to earn money and play hockey and summer in Europe and I wanted to go camping and hiking and make love on the beach. He wanted me to dye my hair blond and get my boobs done and I wanted to wear hoodies and hiking boots. Hell, I would've settled for a damn bike ride once in a while. But that's what happens: if we don't drop dead somewhere around forty-five, we change.

[#]

So. Here I am, back "out there", on the market, at around that age mark.

Pair-bonding is a biological, sociological, and psychological imperative. It increases our chance for survival, for plopping a few more of us on the planet, and historically has been a mechanism to improve one's social standing (insert any one of Jane Austen's books here), and continues to be so today. While the vocabulary of love and desire has existed at least since the ancient Greeks, it wasn't until Shakespeare that love became the transformative higher power that it is today, inspiring risk and change and self-sacrifice. After Shakespeare's *Romeo and Juliet, The Taming of the Shrew, Much Ado About Nothing*, and his wonderful "Sonnet 116":

"Love is not love

Which alters when it alteration finds,

Or bends with the remover to remove:

O no! it is an ever-fixed mark

That looks on tempests and is never shaken"

we started to view matching up with someone as the ultimate goal of our existence, our raison d'être, the pinnacle of our hierarchy of needs, and the reason we keep slogging through life (and, now, online profiles). Almost all forms of art, from the eighteenth and nineteenth century poetry of Barrett Browning and Coleridge to today's meet-cute films and TV romances, have since been feeding that myth. That dream that someday, somehow, that script in the latest rom-com hit will be our life too. It seems to be worse for women, but men fall victim to this ideology too. Think of it. While we've been conditioning our bodies to last another lifetime, we've been conditioning hearts and minds to chase the dream of true, romantic love, to find our one-and-only soulmate, the person who will uplift us spiritually and allow us to fulfill our destiny, for at least six hundred years.

No wonder online dating apps have turned their developers into billionaires.

I've heard it said that dating in midlife is like picking through the bargain bin at the flea market and hoping to find something that looks okay, still works, and doesn't smell too bad. There are reasons these people are still single in their later years. (Hell, there is a reason *I was,* and I should have figured that out long before going "out there" in the first place! But given what happened to me some of this is obviously a "practice what I preach" kind of thing). Basically, the older you are, the more carefully you have to shop, while the pickings get smaller. According to Statistics Canada, about 8% of people between the ages of 45 and 64 reported themselves as single in 2021, across the whole country! So "the One" is the proverbial needle in the haystack.[5]

Dating apps increase the odds, but putting yourself on a dating app for the first time ever after being with one person since college is like walking stark-naked into a stadium full of strangers, knowing that some of them are nice but most could be weird if not dangerous, but having no idea which are which. At least that's what it felt like to me.

Nevertheless, on the advice of my then-therapist, who thought I was too hung up on my dead marriage and needed to live a little, I tried online dating for the first time in my life. Some of you may have been around the block a few times so you'll say I was naive. But maybe some of you are like me, coming out of decades-long relationships with someone who was pretty decent, spending your time working hard, paying off mortgages, putting kids through school, and when you had the time and could afford it, maybe you hit the slopes or went on a road trip somewhere in Europe. Then it all blows up and you find yourself, in your forties, boobs and waist or hairline not where they used to be, and, horrors of horrors, "out there" on the market. And "out there," not everybody thinks like you or the family and friends you've grown up with.

A friend once told me baggage gets bigger as we get older, and we're all coping with some degree of trauma, disorder, or dysfunction. Okay, well, maybe that's another *duh* for you, but it came as a shock to someone emerging from her princess cocoon, and I wish I'd known more about some of this stuff before I put a pic of me smiling big and hugging my horse on a dating app.

A colleague of mine is a researcher in the field of personality types and their disorders. She told me her impression, based on anecdotal evidence at this stage in her research, is that women who had good fathers tend to pick men who are not good to them, whereas women who had not so good fathers all ended up with really good men. Her theory is that women with poor fathers learned at an early age what red flags to look out for in a male partner, and deked left, or right, when they saw them. I, on the other hand, had a great dad. So I guess I never saw Dick Chancer coming.

[#]

The first gentleman who pinged me on the dating app seemed genuinely interested in my equestrian pursuits. We messaged back and forth, his questions to me were eloquent and he seemed to really dig this horsey thing! Even better, he was cute, at least according to his pic, and I was excited! Was I going to be lucky in love so quickly? Then he asked me if it was true what they say about girls who ride horses, and if I was interested in riding *him*. Hum.

There was a very nice man who was living in his wife's basement suite, who was *nothing* like the man I'd been bantering with on the app. I couldn't figure out if he was suddenly shy or if there was a Cyrano de Bergerac in his closet, but the wife's basement thing kind of killed it for me. There was a crane operator who would only call me when he was in the crane and wanted to talk very intimately but never wanted to meet (married much?) There was a dashing man from New Zealand who wore an Indiana Jones hat, with whom I had a great repartee about the impacts of climate change policy, who ghosted me after I refused to go for a kayaking picnic in three-meter waves (okay, maybe there was another reason he ditched me but that was the timeline!). There was a radio station host who was 420-friendly, which he did not mention in our app messaging, and who couldn't wait to end our date when he learned that I had no interest in pot. Which I was okay with, because he couldn't remember my name.

Then there was a very sexy fisherman from Eastern Europe. We went for long walks, he showed me where the salmon used to run before we destroyed their spawning streams, he cooked me dinner, and he was an amazing kisser. He told me how a lot of his friends and family turned their backs on him, that he couldn't understand why, and I felt for his loneliness. But my dog, who loves everybody, didn't like him. She ducked her head every time he tried to pet her. I didn't understand her aversion until one night while having dinner at my house he described, all too graphically, a sexual encounter he had had with a woman he met while in the Algarve, and how the sex had become so vigorous, at the woman's behest according to him, that he had to take her to the hospital. Okay, that was the end of that but this man knew where I lived! I vowed to take my dog on every date in the future, and pay attention to her opinion.

One guy I really liked. We had an online romance for a while to cope with the distance between us and spent many hours video-chatting and flirting. He was a silver-haired, dark-eyed, scientist from out East, recently relocated in BC, who loved to talk about science, the environment, and his cats. Finally, we agreed to meet and I took a ferry across the sea to an island in the Gulf. It was so romantic! But when I got to his place, he made me take a personality test, insisted I stack the dishwasher a certain way, and wouldn't let me sit on the pieces of furniture he had inherited from his mother. Also, his cats were all long dead and he was very particular about his chickens and their eggs. That's okay, I told myself, I like quirky guys who take care of their animals. But when he started swearing at his mother, who wasn't there because she was dead, I fled. Come to think of it, my dog was quite worried about this one too.

My friends have stories as well. One man lost his marriage to his wife's sudden, or so it seemed, onset of depression, leaving him to raise his daughter on his own and piece his life back together. Another friend fell for a woman who was intelligent, beautiful, who taught psychology at school by day and sang with a rock band at night, and who would drink too much sometimes and then text him accusations of being a narcissistic prick. Another friend's husband chronically smoked pot to the point that he couldn't hold a job but after getting half the house and her pension when they split, left her working long hours as a care-aid at the age of 65.

Another friend began dating this guy - handsome, funny, intelligent, had a good job, who, after an LTR and some field-playing, was looking for just the right gal to settle down with when he found her. She thought she'd struck gold. Then, a few days after they'd had (safe) sex for the first time, he tells her that he used to have herpes but due to healthy living and exercise he was all better now so the next time they have sex, they didn't need to use a condom. "Oh, and by the way, don't believe all that shit you'll read on the Internet. I used to have herpes, but I don't anymore."

True enough about the Internet, but "*used* to have herpes"? That's like saying I used to have a brain but decided it was making my head too heavy so I gave it away. While herpes can be prevented and treated, there is no cure! Luckily for this lady, she did still have a brain and promptly dumped this guy and got a blood test. The sex they had was safe so she's okay, but did her golden boy have a few sociopathic tendencies or was he just self-deluded?

No wonder the world is in such turmoil, not just in the post-apocalyptic – oh sorry, I meant the post-separation, next time around, dating market. Unless we're trained in the field, can any of us see the line between an endearing quirk and a disorder?

After all of this I was tired and scared. Scared of being alone and scared of taking a chance. Then, on Valentine's Day, drinking a bottle of wine with my also-single neighbour, I get a message. I almost ignored it, given the online name (Dickalicious? What was that about? My first red flag, that's what) but then he asked about what kind of bike I rode, what my dog's name was, and what my biggest worry was for the environment and the future of the Earth.

After texting back and forth about bikes, when we became vegetarian and why, places we'd traveled to, and the plight of the planet and various endangered species, we arranged to meet. I watched him stride down the street towards me, shaking the spring rain from his shaggy hair, in his cargo pants and Gore Tex jacket, jobless, homeless, and not giving a shit, just ready for the next adventure. A few days and dates later, he was sitting on my couch with my schizophrenic cat, who was terrified of everybody, including me, in his lap, purring like a machine, and my dog, who had been turning herself inside out since she first saw him (her and me both!), lying across his feet. After all the heartbreak, broken dreams, and terrible dates, suddenly there he was. On my couch, in my apartment. Ensconced in my animals and their trust...

The One.

What I learned about Love: Not enough, at this stage, just that the older we get, the harder it is to find.

What you can do: wipe the fairy dust from your eyes before you look for it.

CHAPTER 3: WHAT'S THAT IN YER HAGGIS?

"One day you'll chew off your own foot to get away from me." I said that to my soulmate, the One, aka Dick, very early in our relationship, after we'd bonded over our mutual disgust for our province's horror show they like to call the "wolf cull" and while we were both still in the delirium of newness and pheromone-driven stupidity. His response was an appropriately romantic "Why would you say that? I love you and will love you for all eternity. Now let's get naked..." I had forgotten that moment for years, and it wasn't until a year after we'd blown apart that the grey matter parted and revealed that hidden nugget. And I thought, *whoa, I said that back then, when we were mad for each other? What the hell was that?*

According to doctor of naturopathic medicine, Karen Jensen, we have three brains – the one in our chest, the one in our head, and the one in our guts – and they all have a say in our mental health.[6]You know when you're really torn about something, and there's a buried little niggling, a soft voice from the corner of the rooms of your psyche, saying, *ohnononononono, I wouldn't go there* or *uh-uh, I don't think you want to do that.* Or sometimes it says, *it's time to go, make a change,* or *if you don't do this, you'll regret it forever.*

No, it's not the loud, grating shriek of our fears and anxieties. That's like when you're walking down the gangplank into the belly of an airplane thinking, *geez, is this what cows feel like when they're walking into the slaughterhouse, saying, "Well, moo, Mildred, do you think this is a good idea?" to the bovine next to them,* and you suddenly want to turn around and run away screaming, "Run! Run away for your lives!" What, no fear of flying (are you insane)? What about spiders? Freddy Krueger? The door to the university exam room, the aisle to the altar, the dentist's chair, the zombie apocalypse... That's anxiety. It's also not like the chest-thumping thrill of booking a trip you know you can't afford, or that lurching stomach churn you feel when you first realize you are madly in love with someone. I would describe that as coming from your heart. And it's not the time you balanced the risk between borrowing against your house to pay off your ex or gouging your savings to hold on to your pension—oh wait, did I just give away the ending to this— because that's your brain. Conversely, when we make a decision that "feels right", we can get a sense of clarity and calm. Unlike signals from our brains, signals from the gut, sometimes called intuition, are usually quieter, its advice gentler, but at the same time more pressing. And we ignore it at our peril.

It surprised me to learn about this special connection between the brain and the gut, and I learned it the hard way when I had to go on anti-anxiety meds for the first time in my life (you'll understand why later). Many of these meds are selective serotonin reuptake inhibitors, or SSRIs.

Serotonin is generated in the stomach and used by the brain to transmit messages between neurons. SSRIs increase the levels of serotonin in our system to help us cope with anxiety and depression. We also have what is called a vagus nerve that sends sensory information from the gut to the brain, and motor signals from the brain to your gut. The gut also connects with the brain through other chemicals like hormones and neurotransmitters that also send messages. According to the Cleveland Clinic, the brain and the gut "are like besties[7]", evolving together to help us survive by talking to each other about all kinds of things, from practical matters like what to eat, to emotional ones like who to trust. This is why the gut is sometimes called the "second brain". A brain that can maybe perceive more clearly because it's not driven by sexual and romantic attraction. But its "thinking" is also more diffuse, harder to pick up on, than the cognition from the primary brain in your skull. In other words, you have to still your heart, quiet your skull-brain, and silence your anxieties in order to hear what your gut-brain is telling you.

My sudden, out of the blue, straight from the gut comment to Dick that day was one of those moments. And I ignored it. At my peril...

Or rather I talked myself out of it. Which wasn't hard to do. I had never experienced a connection with anyone - not my mother, not my siblings, not even besties - that compared to what I felt for this man. It really did feel like I had been waiting for him my entire life. Besides, according to some, trusting your gut to the exclusion of your brain is romantic hoo-ha, and blindly following its counsel can set us up for failure[8]. Others say, really, the gut is just full of sh*t.

Meanwhile, Dick was so loving to me and so kind to my dog, and adored *by* my dog, who had been in the past a better judge of character than I was. Most of all, Dick seemed to be as convinced as I was that all the relationship failures we'd had in our respective pasts had been so that we would eventually find each other. Oh wow, how romantic! So this blindly in love engineer lined up the evidence such that it wasn't hard to mistake those churnings in my gut for something else, to turn away from any possible red flag, and toss aside my fears as mere anxiety. On top of that, I was still beating myself up over the failure of my marriage, and was determined to, at least this time, not be the selfish princess I'd been accused of being in the past.

[#]

Guts and brains are not the only thing evolving here. The evolution of family law is a convoluted and tortuous hodgepodge of the efforts of makers of law and policy to keep up with the rapid change of societal norms, roles, and family dynamics. In the era of feudalism, marriage was considered a private affair. That all changed once the Normans came along in 1066, at which point:

> "... the legal status of a married woman was fixed by common law, and canon law prescribed various rights and duties. The result was that the identity of the wife was merged into that of the husband; he was a legal person but she was not. Upon marriage, the husband received all the wife's personal property and managed all the property owned by her. In return, the husband was obliged to support the wife and their children."[9]

At that point, marriage had become a legal entity, and things had to be done according to common law, which means according to the people, and canonical law, which means according to the church. A simple definition for common law is

> "...that it's a "body of law" based on court decisions rather than codes or statutes ...At the center of common law is a legal principle known as stare decisis, which is a Latin phrase that roughly means 'to stand by things decided.' In practice, stare decisis is just a fancy way of saying that courts and judges need to follow earlier decisions and rulings — otherwise known as case law — when dealing with similar cases later."[10]

Meanwhile canon Law is a code of ecclesiastical laws developed within Christianity, particularly in the Catholic Church.[11] Hence the term perhaps: holy matrimony. Vivian Hamilton argues in *The Principles of US Family Law*[12] that family law's "concepts and practices combine in a way that reflect a premodern view of natural law filtered through ... Biblical traditionalism" and "whether our current foundation principles are desirable, or even defensible" because "liberal individualism and Biblical traditionalism are irreconcilable [and the] continued accommodation of both in today's law leads to incoherence..." These institutions once burned women at the stake and claimed they had no soul so expecting laws influenced by their doctrine to be logical and fair may be an exercise in naïveté.

On top of that is the rule of precedence, where courts must decide subsequent cases in line with previous cases. Whether or not things have changed, the genesis of family law hangs around like a vestigial limb, because the expectation is that one member of the union will be dominant financially and the other a dependant, and it doesn't matter if something makes sense or not as long as it's been done before.

Even for those less twitter-pated and more on the ball than I was, it's hard to keep track of all the twists and turns in ever-changing law. Up until the late twentieth century, divorce was only allowed under egregious circumstances in Canada and the United States, such as larceny, violence, and adultery. Only on those grounds could the woman apply to the court for financial relief. If those grounds weren't granted, a woman could lose everything and find herself on the street if she walked away from her marriage. Maybe not so mind boggling when you consider how recently women got the right to vote in these countries.

Canada's first nationwide *Divorce Act* of 1968 was the catalyst for radical changes in all aspects of family law over the next forty years. Now there are three grounds for divorce: adultery, cruelty, and separation. Which means the mere act of being apart for a year means a couple can divorce. And now a lower-earning spouse could finally be free from a bad situation and still be able to put food on the table.

Fast forward a few decades and family law is pressured to change again - to include unmarried (common-law) partnerships, same-sex partnerships, and to better protect the spouses and the children of those partnerships. In response, the province of BC, which had been operating under what it called the *Family Relations Act*, changed to the *Family Law Act* in March of 2013. Under the new act, parental responsibilities were better defined and common-law spouses automatically got exactly the same rights as married spouses – to property division, pensions division, and spousal support. All potentially good things, but what about second or third partnerships, blended families, later in life unions, and relationships with people who break their promises? Are people in those types of relationships also protected by the law? I would one day find out.

But right now, I was more focused on the big shift that was happening in my life, interestingly, at the same time as this legal one. Dick and I had been dating for almost a year, and in March of 2013, the exact same time that BC's FLA came into force, he wanted to go out for dinner. Note that I didn't say, "asked me out for dinner", because I always paid, but at the time, it was wonderfully romantic and I remember the moment so vividly...

We are in a restaurant, celebrating the year gone by since we met online, and after a few beers he tells me that he loves me so much he wants to move in with me. I am terrified. I had only just agreed with my ex-husband on the financials of our divorce. I had only just settled into a small apartment. I had only just euthanized one of my beloved dogs who'd been suffering from a cancer I didn't have enough money to fight, and I was mucking horse stalls to pay the rent. I was still heartbroken but also madly in new love, and, admittedly, pretty drunk on lustful hormones. I felt destitute but had enough money in the bank so I might, just might, buy a new home and be okay. And now he wants to move in with me.

"I can't," I say. "I can't go through it again, what I just went through," telling him about the pain—emotional and financial—

of my breakup with my husband. "It was so awful, so ugly, the lawyers, the anger... I love you, but I can't do it again."

Then Dick stands up in the restaurant, and with tears in his sad blue eyes, with people staring at us, he reaches his arms out toward me and says, "I'd rather live in a hut on a beach in Tamarindo than take a dime from you."

I start to cry and find myself in his arms, saying, "Okay..."

> *"Laws are like cobwebs, which may catch small flies, but let wasps and hornets break through."*—Jonathan Swift

Here's what I learned about the Law: it's always changing, but not always keeping up with the times.

Here's what I learned about Love: your gut instincts are usually right.

What you can do: don't expect justice, in love or in the law, unless you create it yourself.

CHAPTER 4: ARE EWE BEING PETTY?

Dick had a boat and would take me out to sea to look at humpbacks and killer whales. We'd put the kayaks in the water and marvel at the colours of the sea stars, the bizarre yet glistening anemones dangling from the cliffs at low tide, the bears and wolves on the shoreline. I felt like Wendy swept off to Neverland, Meryl Streep in *Out of Africa* wooed by a dashing Robert Redford, Rose falling for Jack Dawson, Lady to Dick's Tramp… It was *so* wonderful. Dick made me feel like the most beautiful, beloved woman of all time, and I quickly became addicted to that feeling. And like an addict, I'd sacrifice just about everything for a fix, especially when it came to my wallet. So off we'd go on another adventure filled with romance and orgasms, and me footing the bill.

But Dick was also away a lot, adventuring on his own or leading ecotours, leaving my gut time to start churning in a different way. Especially after I bought a house.

It was exciting and terrifying – my first house, all on my own! It was an ancient, tiny house that needed a lot of work. I didn't yet have a full-time job, but given the way real estate prices are going in this country, it was a now or never kind of thing. I took a leap of faith and bought that sad, cute, decrepit little thing. Dick would come and go, helping me fix things up a bit when he was in town but the financial burden of the repairs, not to mention a crushing mortgage, were all on me. One day, after Dick had swept back into my life full of adventure stories and horniness, I said...

"I think we should have a cohabitation agreement."

"Oh no, no," he said. "We don't need that. We're in love. I may even marry you someday."

Well, that was the end of that conversation. Yet, I persisted. It took all of my strength, because I was terrified he'd leave me. I spoke to lawyer No. 1, who had helped me with my divorce, about cohabitation agreements, and she expressed some concern over how the new FLA would work. It was so new, no one could predict how it could affect me, especially now that I had a house and Dick made sure all his mail came to its address.

The first draft of the cohabitation agreement (aka cohab, in lawyer-speak) I put in front of Dick basically said you keep your stuff (he had a pension, retirement savings, and owned property) and I'll keep mine, no spousal support. But if you contribute financially to the house, a portion of its equity based on that contribution will be yours. My lawyer and I thought that sounded pretty darn generous given where Dick and I were in life and how we both had stuff we'd gained on our own, before we'd even met.

[#]

The first time I heard about this "gaslighting" thing was during a casual venting with a girlfriend.

"And then he said that in a normal, committed relationship, you share everything, regardless of who pays for what, regardless of circumstances, whether there are kids or not. So now half my house, my savings, my pension, all of which I accrued before I ever met him, should be his. And the only reason I was resisting this was because I don't know how to have a normal, committed relationship. Either that, or I am petty. I've never been called that before... Do you think I'm petty?"

"I don't know," my friend says, "but I do know you've been gaslighted."

"Gaslighted, huh?" I say, nodding my head. I desperately wanted to ask what that was but didn't want to look like an ignoramus. "Like in a bad way?"

Do you have a memory of being terrified of a spider (dog, snake, armadillo... as a child, and one of your parents says, "Oh look, it's just a wee bug...puppy, worm, hairless bunny... (insert harmless creature here, and by the way armadillos are not rodents and are the only living mammal to wear a shell, and are not scary at all!). You can't be scared of that, can you?" Or you say, "I hate bean salad," to which your mother says, "You do not, it's delicious and very good for you." And maybe after enough coaxing and convincing, reluctantly you agree, not wanting to disappoint the person you love most in all the universe? Congratulations, you've been gaslighted.

Gaslighting, unheard of when I started dating in my teens, now is a well-known form of psychological abuse. has a rough rap, but is it always intended to be harmful? How many kids pick up spiders and snakes and think armadillos are cool because of this parental technique? (Me, I love bean salad! And snakes, and armadillos! Thanks, Mom!) Gaslighting can often be unintentional, benign, even arise from good intentions. Be it deliberate or razors in monkeys' hands, at its heart, it is about invalidating how someone feels. According to counsellor-vlogger Christina of *Common Ego*, "regardless of intention—that can leave a mark."[13]

In romantic relationships, gaslighting is usually anything but benign. According to Ramani Durvasula, a clinical psychologist, author, and popular YouTube vlogger, gaslighting is a form of emotional abuse, and both Christina and Durvasula describe it as an instrument of manipulation, often used by people with narcissistic tendencies. Many different phrases and techniques may be used, but it's all about denying how you feel or making you feel stupid, silly, crazy, or—drumroll, please —petty, for feeling what you feel or wanting what you want. Durvasula, Christina, Les Carter, and Stephanie Lynn[14] all have information on narcissism, emotional abuse, manipulation, and gaslighting, so I won't repeat what these experts can tell you. But I how I wish someone had warned me about how gaslighting can hamstring one's efforts to negotiate.

I may have been naiver than most, but I had no idea what gaslighting was when I met Dick. Another "sheep in the headlights" moment the first time he laid it on me. I knew I was upset about the things he was saying—you're so jealous, you're so controlling, that's not what normal committed couples do, etc.— but was always quick to agree with him that it was all my fault. Easier that way because if it's your fault, you can just fix it. Right?

I would one day learn that gaslighting is a technique used by someone who is trying to manipulate you into crossing your own boundaries, and that is almost always wrong. I say *almost always* because not every boundary is healthy. Unhealthy boundaries can be a symptom of an unclear sense of self or needs, such as a people-pleaser to his or her own detriment[15]. Sounds like we've come full circle here: if we have healthy boundaries and someone is trying to convince us to cross them, we are being gaslighted and therefore very likely in an unhealthy relationship; and if we have unhealthy boundaries, we are so prone to people-pleasing that we don't even need to be gaslighted, even if we are in a toxic relationship.

But these boundaries, what the heck are those? Is what I would have said at this stage, which is why Dick was able to convince me to cross them. This is complex stuff that I'm only scratching the surface of, but if it rings a bell, I urge you to get some expert advice.[16] Gaslighting and boundary-crossing are like plastic handcuffs: they may seem pretty harmless and may even come in pretty colours, but they cut pretty deep when you try to resist them. For example, it can sound like this:

"You're going to a party? I rearranged my schedule and cancelled with my friend because we had planned to be together tonight."

"Ya, but I never get to see my friends and so I want to do this instead."

"Am I invited?"

"I guess... but you always want to leave earlier than me and so if you come, I won't have as good a time. Especially when you start saying you want to leave and making me feel guilty if I want to stay."

"I'm upset about this. I thought we had planned to spend tonight together."

"I'm always spending time with you. I never get to see my friends. Don't you want me to see my friends?"

"Of course I do. But couldn't you plan to see them when I'm at work or taking care of my mom, instead of changing plans with me at the last minute?"

"Plan, plan, plan. Why are you so controlling?"

"I'm not... I don't mean to be, it's just that I was looking forward to this and now you're telling me you'd rather be with your friends."

"You're jealous of my friends."

"I'm not... no, I'm sorry, I don't mean to be controlling or jealous. I just... I'm hurt, that's all."

"Don't be so controlling and jealous, and then you won't get hurt."

The last thing may even be said with a hug or a kiss, but the second person in this conversation invalidates the feelings of the first person at every turn, manipulating them until *they* apologize, even though they've been treated improperly. Now that's a skill. Not a nice one, but a skill nonetheless, and a lot of people use it. Like this:

"Okay, so if we're going to live together, we'll need a cohabitation agreement and—"

"Why?"

"Why what?"

"What do we need a cohab for? We're in love, aren't we?"

"Yes but—"

"As in together forever, soulmates… which means we share everything. That's what normal people do when they love each other. That's what *normal* couples do."

"But I'm not sure that's fair. Take that purple vase over there…"

"Ya, I love that vase. Okay, if you want an agreement so badly, which I don't think we need if we're truly in love for forever, but, okay, if you put in the agreement that if we split up, we sell the vase and split the money 50-50, then I'll agree to that."

"But I paid for it. I saved my money. I searched all over for months, looking for just the right one. I had it inspected and valued. My friend helped me buy it. You weren't even in town."

"I dust it sometimes. Oh, and once I stopped the cat from knocking it over. So, there you go, 50-50."

"Um, that's not what I was thi—"

"If you appreciated me as an equal partner, you wouldn't be treating me this way."

"What way? I'm just—"

"Like the way you treated your ex-husband. Unfairly. Right? Isn't that what you told me? And how badly you felt about it, how you wanted it to be different with us? But now you're doing it to me."

"I'm just saying I'd like to split the vase on the basis of financial contribution to its purchase."

"Wow."

"What?"

"You are so petty."

Okay, so maybe a purple vase isn't the hill you want to die on. But what if it's the boat you plan to retire on, or the cottage by the lake with an amazing garden where you plan to write all your steamy romance novels, or the 120-year-old house that you bought all by yourself and worked so hard to renovate and restore? Even then, we could be convinced this is what "normal" couples do—that even when there's no kids, even when we're in our forties or older, when this is our second or third relationship, despite the unequal or complete lack of financial contribution by one partner—those things should be equally shared. And if we push back, are we being petty?

Here's a definition of petty: something that has little or no importance or significance, or of someone caring too much about small and unimportant things, aka "small-minded" or "narrow-minded," to be mean-spirited, or ungenerous, and unkind. I don't know about you, but I'd rather have my appendix, tonsils, and all four wisdom teeth removed—all at the same time and without anesthetic—than have the person I love think any of those things about me. When Dick used that word on me, I crumpled every time. I even went to my own lawyer, this was Lawyer No. 2 now (Lawyer No. 1 had changed provinces, following her own path to love), and demanded that a house-splitting clause be put into our cohab, despite her warning that if the house doubled in value, I would lose it. Some of you may think love is more important than any of those things. All I can say is that's what I told myself too, and later regretted it. Decide for yourself. Just don't be manipulated into it.

[#]

"But he said he's going to marry me," I told my friends.

"But he's getting a full-time job, with a new pension, and he will split that with me. So, it makes sense that, if I get a job with a pension, I should split that with him," I told my family.

"But he said he's going to sell his condo, invest in the house, so it makes sense to split it with him," I told my lawyer.

Dick was working full-time and contributing to a pension when we executed a cohab where I agreed to split my house and my pension. Four months later, Dick quit his job, kept the pension to himself, and never worked again. He didn't sell his condo. Suddenly marriage was out of the question, until I could prove to him that I was worthy of his true love, which meant I had to stop asking him to contribute to our expenses and to stop bitching at him to get a job. Meanwhile, I had signed a one-way ticket to Dick's gravy train.

Oh shit...

Here's what I learned about the Law: it doesn't protect you from empty promises.

Here's what I learned about Love: some people will tell you they love you in one breath, then gaslight you in the next.

What you can do: don't let anyone call you petty.

CHAPTER 5:
AESOP'S TAILS &
MERINO WOLVES

Dick loved to travel and I was able to restore some of the romance by taking him on some trips – Mexico, Hawaii, eco-tours in Desolation Sound – and with promises of more to come once things had stabilized for us. Meanwhile, I was working hard to restore my professional standing, and ended up finding my dream job as an environmental engineer. Even better, it came with a good pension. I could pay for my mortgage, keep up with vet bills, riding lessons, home repairs, and even save for a future that could be financially secure. All with the love of my life. I felt so lucky. Too lucky. Of course, it would be selfish and petty of me to ask Dick to pay for a fair share when I had so much good fortune. It would be tempting fate to take it all away, just like it did when my marriage ended. This was my mantra every time I paid the mortgage, a repair bill, or took out my credit card at a restaurant or to pay for a plane ticket. What's fair anyway, when you're in love and working together towards a rosy future together? Who cares who pays for what? Whose words were those, though, really? Dick's or mine?

This was all hunky-dory for about eighteen months, a typical shelf life for a romance like this.[17] In fact, I've read that the more intense the initial love is, the higher the high, the hotter the burn, the more likely it will turn into a toxic relationship. Long-lasting love is a gentle warming, where you love each other a little more each day, a love built on mutual trust and respect to support all the fun stuff on the ski slopes and in the boudoir. But with a Peter Pan, all you have are the ski slopes and the boudoir, and eventually even that gets old—especially when you're the only one paying for it.

And that's when the first of the Four Horsemen[18] rears his head. I started to criticize, voicing my concerns over Dick not pulling his weight. He struck back, with more guilt trips and gaslighting. "I never said that, I never agreed to that, and you said you were going to do this and that" became Dick's mantra. "I'm sorry" became mine. In his reality, I had promised him we'd go travelling and enjoy life (on my money, of course) within one year of meeting him, and how dare I not keep my promise. What? I had *just* landed the job of my dreams and had *just* mortgaged myself to the eyeballs to buy a house in Vancouver, the third least affordable city in the world after Hong Kong and Sydney[19] while I was supporting the household and trying to afford the trips I did take him on. When he accused *me* of going back on *my* word, I was like, *WTF?* But he said it with those tears in blue eyes that looked at me with such sad intensity, his lower lip trembling in hurt and indignation, that I actually said it again: "I'm sorry."

I tell ya, the guy was good.

Only a few months after the original (and faulty) cohab

was executed, Dick quit his job, cashed in his pension, while I was fully employed with a growing pension and a house that had substantially increased in value. And I started to get a nagging feeling, deep down (there's that gut-brain again), that I was in trouble. Dick never worked full-time again, never sold his condo to contribute to the house, and was now refusing to commit to our relationship on account of my "control issues" and me being "so petty" about money issues. But if I told him to leave, I would lose my home.

Not only was I now trapped financially, I was trapped emotionally as well. What can I tell you, I still loved the guy! I started playing what author and relationship coach Matthew Hussey calls the "One Day Wager."[20] It's the gamble that all the love and effort and giving provided to our loved one will one day pay off, and they will suddenly come to their senses and give us love, respect, and a true partnership. We keep investing in the dream that one day they will become the partner that we want, the one we believe we deserve. Hussey describes it as one of the most dangerous bets we can make because if they aren't that person now, they never will be. But how is that possible? Dick said I was beautiful, he said he loved me like no other, that he'd been waiting for me his entire life, etcetera, etcetera. So, we keep playing, rolling the dice, going all in, because one day we have to come up aces, right? Until the one day we wake up with a broken heart and an empty wallet.

> *"Happiness... is a perpetual possession of being well deceived."*
> —Jonathan Swift

Researching this book and looking for fun facts about

sheep, I came across some of Aesop's fables.[21] Aesop loved to use stereotypes about animals to tell his stories, not all of which stand the test of time, but still – it's amazing that this Aesop guy lived almost three thousand years ago and yet the morals of some of his fables resonate today. Like *The Lion, the Bear, & the Fox* (those who do all the toil do not always get the profit) and the one called *The Wolf and the Lamb*. While I protest Aesop's habit of denigrating wolves, the moral of this fable – about a wolf drumming up excuses to justify his killing of a young lamb who protests her innocence, is just too apt: a tyrant will always find a pretext for his tyranny, and it is useless for the victim to ask for justice when the other intends to be unjust.

One night, after taking Dick out for dinner and being told yet again that my behaviour was preventing him from committing to our relationship, I told him that, given the new circumstances we needed a new agreement. One that honours his desire for freedom and my greater financial contributions to the house. We'll draft something where you can contribute as much or as little as you like, I said, and if we do split, (*I sounded cool but was dying inside at the prospect!*) the division will be in proportion to those contributions.

Dick wasn't having it. At first, he tried to get me to back down by walking out the door. Devastated and scared, I went to a new lawyer, Lawyer No. 3, on advice from a counselor, to find out what I was in for. Emotionally I was already a wreck, but what about financially?

"It's not great," No. 3 told me. "I just finished a settlement with a woman in a similar situation. Her house is up for sale now so she can pay out her ex. Are you sure this relationship is over?"

Well, not according to my tears and heartbreak it certainly wasn't. And Dick wasn't yet done with me either. It was now December, and I tried to distract myself with family and friends and preparation for Christmas. One night, after it had started to snow, I went out with a friend for a glass of wine (okay, more than just one), and I get a text from Dick, telling me he is homeless, and he's cold.

[#]

Initially, I reached out to make sure Dick wasn't going to freeze to death, but I ended up accepting his proclamations of true and forever love. Dick moves back into my house. Our new agreement was drafted by a junior associate at Lawyer No. 3's firm - Lawyer No. 4 - who has a focus on collaborative law. Dick and I are reconciling, right? So I want to collaborate, right?

No. 4's draft reads more like the agreement I had in mind in the first place, where we share the house based on the money we put towards its purchase and upkeep, which made perfect sense to me. It gives Dick the freedom he says he wants, especially when it comes to employment, or lack thereof, and how he spends his money, or lack thereof. And it gives me a share of the house commensurate with all the money I've poured into it. (So focused on keeping my house, I forgot about my pension, which wasn't worth all that much at this time, another mistake I will regret!) At the time, this new agreement seemed to solve everything we've been fighting about. But Dick keeps saying he doesn't understand it. Or could you please ask your lawyer to redraft this bit. Or I need to ask my lawyer about that bit. Or sometimes he says he's tired and could he read it later. Or sometimes he distracts me with an offer to drink some wine and get naked. But mostly it's that he keeps saying he doesn't understand it.

This confuses me. Despite his claims to be penniless and homeless at times, Dick is an educated, clever man. He certainly understood the first agreement, where he got half my house and my pension. What's going on now? Why won't he sign it?

Still believing, or trying to believe, that Dick and I are a love meant to be if only we can stand the trials we now face, I decide to try to find out what could be going on behind those sad blue eyes and his inability to comprehend and sign this new agreement, which to me seems to be the answer to all of our woes. I was being an engineer, an engineer who still loved her Dick, flaws and all, and determined to find a way to make her soulmate dreams come true. First, we identify the problem. Research followed by problem-solving. Hurrah. All that listening to your gut stuff is just hogwash. All I had to do was to understand what made my Dick tick. And then he will sign a more fair agreement and we'll finally get back to the business of living happily ever after.

[#]

The last thing I want to do is to stigmatize or be disrespectful towards people coping with a personality disorder or a mental health issue. But because of this research, along with guidance from a Very Brilliant Psychologist (VBP), I now know what at least some of my issues are, and how they led me into the pickle I found myself in with Mr. Chancer. Dr. Theodore Millon wrote a book called *Personality Disorders in Modern Life,*[22]which I would now call recommended reading before putting oneself on any dating app. The book includes scenarios and character studies, and a succinct summary table based on the *Diagnostic and Statistical Manual of Mental Disorders*[23], also referred to as the "DSM" in psychiatric practice. Meanwhile, here are some of the issues, tendencies, or conditions – including physical and psychological, and not all are personality disorders - that I researched in my efforts to figure out why Dick was treating me the way he was.

Sociopaths and psychopaths: are terms for what psychiatry calls antisocial personality disorder. Despite what Hollywood says, people with these disorders are not necessarily violent, although they can demonstrate a lack of regard for the safety of others, or be unremorseful. Many people demonstrate deceptive traits, lack of regard for others, and manipulate for their own gain, but can we see the line between that and a disorder? I'm not sure why I looked into this one. Maybe it was my romance with a guy whose cats were all dead. Or the woman's with a guy who "used to have" herpes.

Covert misogyny (or ***misandry*** if it's a prejudice against men): Dr. Millon may have categorized this as *Amorous Narcissism*. When you first meet them, they are all lovely and charming, but their past is littered with a long trail of sexual partners, quickly used and tossed aside, and can involve a disguised hatred of one's opposite sex. Dick had a lot of ex's and adored Woody Allen and thought Harvey Weinstein got a bad rap, which is why I looked into this.

Attachment Issues: Dick, who hadn't had a relationship that lasted longer than a year, hated his still-living father yet adored his dead mother. So I looked into "attachment issues", which are linked to issues around our primary caregivers carried over from childhood, have been described as a subset of borderline personality disorder (BPD) by some researchers,[24] and can lead to difficulties in maintaining relationships. In some pop media, this has been referred to as *Mommy/Daddy Issues*.

But none of these really resonated so I also looked into some medical conditions to explain things.

Depression & Dementia: Not to medically link these in any way, but both can be subtle, especially in the early stages of a relationship. The sad thing is that someone you love can also develop such a condition over time and as a result suddenly decide, through no fault of your own, that they can no longer function in a relationship with you. Onset of depression or dementia can rip your heart and your family apart. Even if you want to stand by your partner and weather this terrible illness together, sometimes they just leave and there's nothing you can do. I include these here because both run in Dick's family and so I wondered – is this what he was dealing with and acted the way he did? (It wasn't).

Brain injury: The grisly story of Phineas Gage is perhaps the most famous of this type of injury. Phineas Gage was a twenty-five-year-old railroad worker in 1848 when an errant explosion drove a four-foot tamping iron through his skull, ripping out a good chunk of his frontal lobe. He miraculously survived and lived another decade, reportedly losing some of his previous inhibitions, before a seizure took his life.

But it doesn't have to be a wound so extreme. We know so much more about the risks and long-term effects of concussions and other brain injuries than we did, say, twenty years ago. Which means that someone who toughed out a severe concussion in their thirties or forties, thinking that was the thing to do, could be in for some trouble as they hit middle age today. For example, someone who suffered a frontal lobe injury could experience reduced reasoning and problem-solving skills, poor judgment, and impulse control, and start engaging in risky or inappropriate behaviors such as drug use or unsafe sex practices.[25]

Brain injury doesn't always even involve physical trauma. Long-term cannabis use, especially by adolescent males, has been linked to "alexithymia, multiple signs of frontal lobe dysfunction in everyday life, and impulsivity."[26] Alexithymia is defined as the difficulty in recognizing and expressing emotions, which can make someone seem unempathetic, uncaring, even narcissistic. Meanwhile, other studies have indicated that cannabis has wonderful medicinal properties[27] for people suffering from chronic pain or disease, although the same researchers often say more study is needed on long-term effects. I live in BC, where smoking pot is a way of life for many, but do the 420 friendlies notice any long-term changes in their brains and behaviour? And if they did, would they care? This was yet another alley I went down, after seeing how hooked on Facebook Dick was was, after I'd heard about an untreated concussion, and after a mutual friend told me he smoked up a lot in high school. (Then again, anything that's "a lot" apparently isn't good for you. Even wine. And double-fudge, caramel, Oreo ice cream. I know, insert shocked and sad emoji's here.)

I even looked into autism. Some people in my family are on the spectrum, and they are talented, interesting people who see the world in new and unique ways. Perhaps that's why Dick and I viewed fairness oppositely - I wanted a partnership where we both contributed what we could, and he wanted me to pay for everything because I had the higher salary. In the end nothing quite fit, or quite explained why Dick could do all the things he could do – navigate a boat, read complex books, balance his taxes - and yet be unable to commit to a relationship, hold down a job, nor understand an agreement where he receives based on what he put in.

I kept looking, reading, talking to friends, until that very brilliant psychologist (VBP) told me about something called...

Peter Pan/Lost Boy Syndrome: These are people, usually men, who have the body of an adult but the mind, psyche, or emotional intelligence of a teenager. Psychologist Dan Riley[28] coined the term *Peter Pan syndrome* in his attempt to explore and explain the behaviours of these men who refuse to grow up. Frequently linked to narcissism, this syndrome is more common than we'd like to think, especially when we're on the wrong side of forty and looking at who else is left standing on the "still single" side of the playing field.

Research into this syndrome led me to learn about...

Covert or vulnerable narcissism:[29] Another member of the Cluster B family of personality disorders, one that can be a very well-camouflaged disorder. Unlike the more common and better-known overt narcissists, who are flagrant, grandiose, or malignant in their narcissism (like a certain US president), vulnerable narcissists tend to be introverted, seemingly respectful, helpful, quiet, and are often described as "sweet."

They will injure you the same way an overt narcissist does, but you never see it coming so you tend to blame yourself. In the end, you will also be blamed for absolutely everything by the vulnerable narcissist, who deflects all blame and can't take responsibility for anything, probably due to some deep sense of shame and inadequacy, so you can end up in a toxic stew of anxiety and self-doubt. Meanwhile, all narcissists, including vulnerable ones, have a sense of entitlement to things they have not earned. Like love, respect, and money. Their behaviour in relationships tend to follow a pattern,[30] where they do something called "love-bombing" in the beginning, where they tell you that you are the most amazing, gorgeous, lovely person they have been looking for their entire life, followed by devaluation, where they criticize your appearance, your values, your friends, and so on. They may even call you petty. After this stage, a narcissist will often discard the person they once claimed to love so much, and go in search of a new supply of sex, money, or whatever feelings you once gave them.

Dr. Million also discussed variations of some of these disorders. Of note for me were:

The Covetous Antisocial: "...individuals feel that life has not given them 'their due'; they have been deprived of their rightful amount of love, support, or material reward; and others have received more than their share. Jealous of those who have received the bounty of a good life, they are driven by an envious desire for retribution to take what destiny has refused them."

The Nomadic Antisocial – "...see themselves as jinxed or doomed and desire only to exist at the edge of a world that would almost certainly reject them. Mired in self-pity, they drop out of society to become gypsy-like roamers, vagabonds, or wanderers. With little regard for their personal safety or comfort, they may drift from one setting to another..."

The Amorous Narcissist: "...[entices and tempts] the emotionally needy and naïve, while fulfilling their own hedonistic desires and sexual appetites as they deem necessary. Although their game plan usually implies the possibility of an exclusive relationship, they are not inclined toward genuine intimacy, instead choosing to romance a number of potential conquests simultaneously. Some are sexual athletes whose designs call simply for sexual exploitation. They may seem to desire the warm affection of a genuine relationship, but when they find it, they usually feel restless and unsatisfied.

Learning about these last two conditions felt like someone dumping a very large, very cold, bucket of ice water over my head.

[#]

If we can recognize these tendencies in ourselves, as well as our romantic partners, will we be better prepared, than I was, when it all inevitably comes up like an iceberg slicing into the *Titanic* once the blush is off the rose, love has bit the dust, and the shit has hit the fan (and yes, I was trying to see how many clichés I could fit into one sentence)?

I'm not sure - relationships are dynamic and fluid and sometimes people change. And sometimes they were always a wolf wearing merino. I say that with an apology and with all due respect to wolves. I love wolves. They are incredible, beautiful animals with strong familial bonds and tremendous intelligence. Our species horribly persecutes them and that needs to stop. But wolves are also really good at manipulating and hiding from their prey, so the analogy is apt. What I'm saying is, once we start googling these disorders, that could be our gut telling us something really is wrong, and it's probably something we can't fix.

"*I never wonder to see men wicked, but I often wonder to see them not ashamed.*"— Jonathan Swift (I love this guy)

What I learned about Love: that I was desperate enough for it to be my own undoing.

What you can do: Listen to your gut, not your Dick, who's probably wearing a really nice, soft fleece sweater.

CHAPTER 6:
LAMB STEW

Any gender can have a personality disorder or mental health issue, but the later-in-life dating scene is particularly challenging for women for several reasons. For one thing, it is still easier for a man to find someone willing to be with him no matter how old he is, especially if he has money. According to the dating site Zoosk, 60% of men want a younger woman, while only 27% say they'd date an older one.[31] A 2018 study indicates that a man's sexiness peaks at age fifty, while a woman's peaks at eighteen.[32] Yeah, you read that right. Eighteen! If that's Mother Nature, then she really is a bitch.

Sometimes, and certainly in some places, it just sucks to be a girl. Women's pickings are slimmer. That's just a sad fact. If a woman is lucky enough to find someone who doesn't care about her age, it's likely because she has something else that they want, like a nice savings account, or a boat, or a house in a tight market like Toronto's or Vancouver's (hello!). Unlike the era in which family law came onto the scene, women now are more likely than ever before to have the status and financial wherewithal that was once almost the exclusive purview of men. And that's only been in the past few decades. No wonder family law has such a hard time keeping up. No wonder so many women put themselves in an emotionally and financially vulnerable position. I guess I'm writing this for the former me, the wide-eyed babe in the woods entering a scary new world of relationships, and telling her to be as careful and choosy as she can be. But even if men have more options, anyone looking for love is vulnerable.

[#]

Okay, so maybe Dick was a Peter Pan, a Lost Boy with a heavy side of vulnerable narcissism (most Peter Pans are, apparently[33]), and we met when his desirability was peaking whereas I, almost thirty years on the wrong side of eighteen, was way past it (I still can't get over that). He had made some poor choices in life, including throwing away a lucrative career to go yachting and do drugs with twenty-somethings. When that didn't work out so well, he washed up on some foreign shore and spent all his savings while banging tourists and bongos on the beach. Of course, he had great reasons – dead friends, lost loves, broken hearts - but the one I fell for was that his mother had died, too young, how profoundly affected he was by her loss, and went off to live the life she never had, traveling the world the way she never could. Suddenly what had seemed like a bunch of flaky choices was transformed into a tragic, romantic, hero's journey! They all have these great stories, Peter Pans. Heroic or flaky, I'll let you decide, but now this Pan had washed up on *my* shore, bedraggled and lost and adorable. Like a drowning puppy, I had to save him, my poor, sweet cute Lost Boy. I just had to because I, even though I didn't realize yet, am a Wendy.

Yes, there's one personality disorder I was about to

discover: the Wendy syndrome, the flip side, the woman behind the Pan, enabling his immature choices and behaviours. Because Peter Pans can be so much fun! Dick was audacious, adventurous, and naughty, blowing off his commitments so we could drink wine and tipsily career down rain-slick streets on our bikes in the middle of the night, and come home to make love on a Monday when most people our age were tucking their kids in or preparing for the next workday. We smoked pot on the beach. Skinny-dipped in the lake. Made love in the forest. Snuck aboard the yachts he worked on and made love in them too. It was the twenty-something romance I had missed because I got married so young to a man who made me feel safe rather than truly alive.

Apparently, Wendy will kill for that shit. As Greek school psychologist Georgia Kiziridou wrote in 2018:

"Most people are aware of the Peter Pan syndrome: the eternal child who refused to grow up and assume his/ her responsibilities. However, Peter Pan could never exist without Wendy who supports and reinforces him. Wendy represents all the insecure women who are involved in an unequal relationship with the opposite sex, who do anything so that they don't end up alone. Women like these have low self-esteem and constantly sacrifice their personal needs by taking care of an... immature man. They sacrifice their needs with so much dedication with the intent to control their partner, thus designating how essential they are in this relationship... It is said that children that have not received unconditional love within their own family are the ones with the Wendy syndrome... in order to fight their fear of rejection and abandonment. The more intense, deep and unconscious

the emotional gaps are within their parental family, the more intense the need to... take care of each of their partners is."[34]

Yup - the eldest daughter of an uber-religious mother who was told as a child that she was full of sin, who felt the typical first-born pressure to succeed and hold everyone's shit together, judged at every turn, and abandoned when her dad couldn't take it anymore and left—I am a Wendy.[35] No wonder when Dick and I first met and he told me how sad he was (dead marriage, dead mom, yolo, yolo, yolo, or "You lonely live one", an excuse I often heard) and how he needed to chuck everything to heal his broken heart and I offered to buy his lunch that—*clang, clang, clang*—the bells of mad, crazy love went off for both of us. Peter Pan had come back from his travels, jobless, homeless, and with emptied pockets, and needed a Wendy. And he found me, searching for the Lost Boy of her dreams.

[#]

For years Dick and I adhered to the new agreement, where he paid less towards our life together and had more freedom – which is what he wanted. But kept finding excuses not to sign it, and I kept finding excuses to accept his promises that eventually he would.

So what if Dick is a little immature - I loved his playfulness. So what if he wouldn't get a job - it meant he could spend more time with me. So what if I was burning through my savings paying for stuff - that's what people do when they're in love, and on the excuses went. Because I wasn't ready to wake up from my dream of happily-ever-after. There had to be a reason why our love was falling apart, why Dick had stopped saying I love you all the time, why he looked at me funny sometimes, almost like he was disgusted. If I could figure it out, I could just fix it, right? I just needed to be more understanding, figure out where he was coming from. Not to mention lose the weight I'd gained from stress-eating all the time. And then maybe we could sign a new agreement that would work for both of us. So, he'd start calling me Babe again and I could stop being so petty and controlling and... and... angry.

What Dick was doing, and had been doing for years, put him in a position of great power. "With great power comes great responsibility," according to Stan Lee, writing about Spider-Man. Dick didn't like responsibility very much yet he still had tremendous influence over almost everything I did. Despite my job, owning the house, having more money, Dick reigned supreme because he did this one extremely formidable thing. Do you know what it was?

Nothing. He did absolutely nothing.

I believe Dick knew he had me by the ovaries because of the effed-up cohab I signed when blinded by love and gaslighting. And now, no matter how much I tried to explain, to appease, to reason, to compromise, to offer solutions, no matter how desperately I begged him to see that the situation was unfair to me, no matter how many drafts my lawyer (No. 4) wrote of the new cohab, no matter how many different calculations I did to show him that he was still getting a fantastic deal, Dick just sat there and watched me boil in my own juices. Stonewalling, John Gottman calls it, the last of the four horsemen before a relationship ends, which may also be a form of gaslighting.[36] If someone's concerns are frequently dismissed or ignored, they start to devalue themselves and their principles, and maybe even their own reality.[37]

All I know is Dick had absolute control by doing absolutely nothing and, maybe, at least to some extent, he enjoyed watching me squirm. I was jumping through all the hoops like a border collie at a super-dog show and why was nothing happening? I didn't know this was a sign my relationship was over.

It was quite a shock when I realized that I was angry. Really *angry*. Because not only had my ewe been culled but now my lamb was stewed! Oh sure, there was still lots of fun and adventure and great sex, but when I wasn't laughing or having orgasms, I was really effing mad. Like, all the time. Meanwhile, Dick was often so sweet and nice and helpful, so I'm thinking, *What the hell is wrong with me?* Between this and Dick's gaslighting, I really did start to feel like I was losing my marbles.

Harriet Lerner, the author of the illuminating, groundbreaking book *The Dance of Anger*[38], writes that anger, which we, especially women, have been taught to suppress, is a signal. And an important one that, like our gut, we ignore at great risk. Anger means your boundaries have been crossed, she writes, and when that happens, we get upset or anxious or resentful, and *angry*. But we often don't know why... So we ask ourselves, *Why am I so angry? Am I selfish? Am I petty?* No, we are not, but we haven't been taught how to take our cues from that anger, how to listen to it and understand where it comes from. We are taught, especially women, that to be angry is to be a bitch, so most of us push that anger down and swallow it, until we're choking on our own poisonous juices.

So. Boundaries... What the hell are those? At that point in my life, I wouldn't have known a boundary if I slammed up against one and broke my nose on it. But we all have them, whether we realize it or not, no matter how buried they are beneath our desires to get along and be loved. And when the people in our lives cross them, we get mad, in that deep, awful, gut-twisting way—when you are really upset about something but don't know why or think you shouldn't be and try hard to convince yourself you're totally okay with it even though you are totally not! This can go on for years and years, until you either break away from your boundary-crosser or die of a stress-induced disease. Or jump off a bridge, drive your car through a stranger's house, or cut off a penis. Not to justify any of those things, but long-suppressed anger can make anyone go berserk.

According to author and researcher Brené Brown, boundaries – basically rules that we make for ourselves on what is okay for us versus what is not okay[39] – should be based on our values, and she shares a list of what those look like on her coaching site *Dare to Lead*, named after her bestselling book.[40] She suggests picking your top ten or fifteen values from this list, and try setting some boundaries from there, boundaries that will prevent resentment and potentially save our relationships. A few that lit up for me were *Honesty, Integrity, Achievement, Accountability, Commitment, Responsibility, Stewardship...* Hmmm ...

Okay, as worrisome as that was, at that point I figured, all I had to do was set some boundaries and everything would be okay! Starting with my house. I know these days that we're all not so lucky to have one, but I grew up in my houses and I've always loved them dearly—all their creaks and quirks and ugly carpets—and I've pined like I've lost a friend or sibling when I've had to leave them. Selling the house I'd had with my husband, which had been a wreck and lovingly restored, ripped my heart out, especially when the new owners tore it down—an old house from a bygone era—to put up a set of concrete slabs. I still can't bear to go down the street where that house once stood. When I was so lucky to buy this little ancient thing that had once been a grow-op and give it another chance, well, it was like coming home. I was willing to share my house but not give it away. I was willing for it to be a family home, not a bag of money for someone to cash in on someday, especially not someone who didn't pay for it. But hell's bells and gaga in love, I had signed a cohab without realizing that I was also signing off on a free pass for Dick to cross my boundaries. And that turned out to be a huge and very costly mistake that drove me crazy with anxiety and turned me into one very stressed-out, stress-eating, somewhat overweight, lady.

Truth was my relationship was over long before I was ready to see it. The saying goes that you fall out of love very slowly, then all at once. So slowly, in my case, that when the "all at once" came, it was a horrific gut-wrencher of a shock. Oh sure, my gut-brain (that damn thing again) had been telling me for years that this relationship was a one-way highway to hell, but my Wendy wasn't listening, was she? Over the next few years, even though we were still having hot sex and grand adventures, I had constant nightmares about Dick disappearing, turning his back on me, showing up with a new woman, disappearing down a road and leaving me abandoned in dark places. The next day would be full of love, kisses, a pancake breakfast, a trip to the beach, wine, hot sex... but I knew. At least the brain in my gut knew, if only it could have convinced the one in my head.

Sidebar, Your Honour: Paying attention is always important in a relationship, to yourself and your partner, not just when it's dying. If you are in a good, healthy relationship, *especially* if you are in a good, healthy relationship, you need to pay attention.

Sustained - Nothing is more dreadful than the sentence that starts with "If only I had..." long after the love of your life has walked out the door. Obviously, that's tragic. But in my case, Dick's withdrawal was inevitable. Because Peter Pans, according to the experts, [41] are generally incapable of healthy, long-term relationships unless they make big strides in maturing during one.

What finally ended things, for good this time was this: After I had taken him on an all-expenses-paid trip to a tropical paradise for his birthday, I quickly discovered three things. A property assessment that indicated my house had dropped in value. A letter from Dick's pension office saying he could start taking payments anytime. And that Dick had booked himself a trip to the Caribbean. Seriously? If he could afford that, why had I been paying for everything? Worse than that, why wasn't I invited? I mean, it's a relatively innocent thing. People go on trips all the time without their partners. But for some reason, for me, that was it. I snapped.

Sign the amendment, I said, or don't come back from your holiday. In hindsight, I think it was a Hail Mary pass on my part, one last-ditch effort to stand up for my boundaries, to get him to come to his senses and treat me more fairly so I could stop being so anxious and angry and stop smoking and maybe lose some weight and then we could live happily ever after...

Except this time, he didn't come back...

Here's what I learned about the Law: It can't protect our boundaries if we don't know what they are.

Here's what I learned about Love: Not knowing our boundaries, or being unable to stand up for them, can kill a relationship.

What you can do: Learn to love yourself first and best, before you try to love someone else.

CHAPTER 7: UNRAVELLED

There's a great saying floating around the Internet: "A bad relationship is like standing on broken glass. If you stay, you will keep hurting. If you walk away, you will hurt but eventually you will heal." But for me the price for freedom would turn out to be a tortuous path. First up was the storm of grief, anger, loss, and post-trauma that whirled through me like a tornado.

Sidebar Your Honour – by now you must be thinking, Wendy or not, this lady is just a stubborn idiot practically begging to be taken advantage of. Who, *mind* you, gave Dick a very angry, aggressive ultimatum just when her house dropped in value. So not only did he have no choice but to leave, she was actually very calculating about it.

Overruled. I did find the courage to finally stand up for a boundary when house prices had dropped, but my house had still increased in value, and Dick could still, under the previous cohab, claim hundreds of thousands of dollars. Besides, by that time, I was so distraught, not only by losing my fantasy island with my perfect soulmate, but by the realization that friends and family were indeed correct and that I'd been used - Dick left when his pension checks had started rolling in, he had cashed in on his condo, and he didn't need me anymore. I was torn up with so much grief and rage, I couldn't think straight. Even my gut-brain went AWOL, and I made several *more* mistakes I will tell you about in the hopes that you don't make them too.

Truth be told, I was already pretty unravelled long before the legal battle even began.

Seven years, almost to the day. They talk about the "Seven-Year Itch." Articles are written about it,[42] Marilyn Munroe starred in a movie about by the same name; it's the time between the start of big love to where you start to get restless and want to make a change. When I married my husband, we called it the "Seven-Year Hitch" because we'd been living together that long and it was either break up or get married. My relationship with Dick lasted just shy of seven years. It was exactly how long it took me to finally have enough of Dick and his shenanigans, but also the time it took for me to become an unrecognizable version of myself. An angry, controlling, anxiety-ridden, stress-eating bitch. It was only when I realized that I hated what I had become more than what he was doing to me, that I finally found the strength to show him the door, and the courage to fight for what I felt was right, for my house, and for my future. I should have listened to my gut and asked him to leave years ago. I can't tell you how desperately I wish I could have those seven years back, and I wondered who and where I'd be if I had them.

Even if we learned how to recognize gaslighting techniques and emotional manipulation, what can we do about it? I won't repeat what the experts can tell you, but we do get to decide whether or not we continue with this relationship. As I indicated earlier, not all gaslighting is malignant or intentional.

Therapist Les Carter points out in one of his videos[43] that gaslighters are usually lying to themselves before they start to gaslight you, and that it's often a defence mechanism used by people with egos too fragile to face their mistakes or failures. So they construct an alternate reality where they are the standard-bearers of kindness and decency, where all their other relationships are perfect, or where they are always in the right and the only problem they have is with you...

How could I have ever thought I could fix that?

I also learned that gaslighting and other forms of emotional abuse can lead to something called a trauma bond[44] —yet another thing I'd never heard of when I fell for Dick. Patrick Carnes introduced this concept in 1997 in his book *The Betrayal Bond: Breaking Free of Exploitative Relationships*[45] and an example is the infamous *Stockholm Syndrome*, named for what happened to Patty Hearst, who was kidnapped, abused, and (allegedly) fell in love with one of her captors and joined his cause.

According to retired clinical psychologist John Tholen, quoted in *Forbes* magazine, trauma bonds are characterized by cycles of abuse and kindness. One minute they're calling you their soulmate and they will love you for all eternity; the next they're calling you petty, dishing out the insults, or worse. And that can lead to something called cognitive dissonance, which is the perception of contradictory information and the attempts to cope with the resulting anguish. Crossing personal boundaries can also lead to cognitive dissonance, as can being in love with someone who abuses you.

"While it's hard to believe that people can develop affection for an abuser, trauma bonding is an example of the extremes to which a person's subconscious mind will go in order to reduce inconsistencies between their beliefs and experiences."[46]

Trauma bonds[47] can be created from a cycle of love-bombing and abuse, which can be in the form of passionate declarations of love and romantic adventures followed by criticism, manipulation, and gaslighting, all of which can create a dependency and addiction to the cycle of highs and lows. These extremes are one reason why a trauma bond is also a power imbalance, which can lead to exploitation. In my case, on the surface it looked like I had all the power – I had more money, the job, the house we are both living in — but in reality, I had no power at all. While I didn't experience anything as horrific as physical abuse or kidnapping, Dick exploited my desperate need for the unconditional love I'd never had, and then managed to, with gentle stealth, cut me from my herd of family and friends, make me completely emotionally reliant on him, and then proceeded with gaslighting and emotional and financial abuse to get what he wanted. I kept giving in because I felt that if I broke the connection to him, it would destroy me.

I wasn't wrong. When that bond *was* suddenly severed, it was an injury with a pain I'd never had before—and I've been stepped on by horses, sprained ankles, broken my back, my knee, my pelvis, and had a burst appendix! Even though the relationship was over, I felt addicted to the person who had mistreated me, to the love and the happily ever after dream he snatched away when I didn't do what he wanted, but also the drama that the relationship, toxic as it was, created in my life. Without it, everything felt flat and bleak. I felt lost, as if life has no purpose or meaning. I experienced greater anxiety than ever before. I lost twenty pounds, couldn't sleep, couldn't stop crying, wondering if I had made a terrible mistake. The pain was so severe, I found myself, I'm embarrassed to say, begging Dick to come back, just so it would stop.

But of course, he didn't. Dick was cool, calm, and just waiting to collect. He was savvy enough to wait a few months, and then I got an email asking how I was and if my emotions had subsided enough to talk about what I owed him. This was followed by him agreeing to meet, where he showed great emotion (those trembling lips and sad blue eyes again!) where he said we could re-establish contact once I'd paid what I owed him. When I found the strength to walk away, this was quickly followed by a letter from a lawyer telling me I owed Dick hundreds of thousands of dollars.

I freaked, and called Lawyer No. 4...

"He said I had hurt him so deeply. But maybe at some point we could have a glass of wine and talk."

"And then what," Lawyer No. 4 said.

"Well, he said we should settle up and then maybe he'll be able to talk to me again, to try to feel the way he used to feel."

"Oh my God, he's fucking with you."

"What? No, that can't be true! He cried!"

But after a few more sessions with that VBP, after a few

more friends came forward with how they really saw things, and after my dad said...

"The guy's bent. Bent on using you. I saw it from the beginning, but you were so in love with him, I had to bite my tongue. But now? Tell that &%$# to go piss up a rope!" And that was it. Even though it was still terribly hard to let go, even though I was still in love with the guy - in some weird, twisted, trauma-bonded kind of way - I had finally had enough. Enough of Dick's love and larceny and my excusing it.

On my instruction, my lawyer sent back a letter suggesting Dick urinate upwards along something made of twisted hemp, but in that nice, convoluted, legal language they use so you're never quite sure how upset you should be. Okay, okay, I had also learned that Dick had gone to Mexico to be with another woman about a month after we'd gotten back from the vacation I'd paid for, but the point is, I could finally see what the relationship really was, who Dick really was. Then all that grief turned into rage. My lamb may have been stewing and boiling over at times during the relationship, but now it was charbroiled over red-hot flames.

As painful and horrible as it is to admit, I finally had to face the truth about my fairy tale – my Prince Charming was essentially a con artist and I'd been had.

Here's the Recap:

What I learned about the Law:

It has evolved to protect the lower-earning spouse, regardless of the circumstances.

It's always changing, but not always keeping up with the times.

It doesn't protect you from empty promises.

It can't protect our boundaries unless we know what they are.

What I learned about Love:

That's it's really hard to find.

But not worth being so desperate for it that we are our own undoing.

The sooner we stand up for our boundaries, the safer we'll be, whether or not the relationship survives.

What you can do:

Learn the basics of family law in your jurisdiction before moving in with anyone.

Check in with a family lawyer before letting anyone move in with you.

Learn your values and boundaries before letting anyone move in with you.

When negotiating something that's important, don't let anyone call you petty.

Listen to your gut, not your Dick (or Dickette).

Love yourself first and best before trying to love another.

PART TWO: INTO THE CHUTE

CHAPTER 8: TERMS OF A SHEARING

First, I was blindsided by love. Now I was about to be blindsided by the law. I had a signed cohab agreement, but it wasn't written in a way that protects a Wendy from a Peter Pan who turns into a Dick. I had attempted to remedy this with an amendment, which we operated under for several years before Dick told me: "I was never going to sign that thing." Now he was demanding an outrageous sum of money and half my pension, and if I didn't pay, he'd go after spousal support to boot.

Sorry Your Honour, but please – First this lady turns herself inside out trying to make a relationship work with a dude who may, or may not, have been an abusive dick, but was certainly taking advantage of her. And now she consults with thirteen lawyers trying to fight back. Not one, not two, but thirteen! Were they all telling her the same thing and she just couldn't accept it? What's that famous insanity quote from Albert Einstein – that the "definition of insanity is doing the same thing over and over again and expecting different results"?

Not Guilty. There's a difference between a pathological, persistent repeating of words and action, and perseverance, which is a "steady persistence in a course of action in spite of difficulties, obstacles, or discouragement.[48]"

Persistent. Not insane. Let's go with that.

> *"Success is not final; failure is not fatal: It is the courage to continue that counts"* – Winston Churchill

All couples deciding to split have big decisions ahead around three basic things: How to divide the stuff (real estate, savings, pensions, etc.) that you both have, how to support and parent any children you may have, and how to support the lower-earning spouse[49].

That means these are all things to consider when planning a cohabitation and any agreements that will govern it. Maybe that sounds too dry to describe your happily ever after. All I'll say at this point is that if my cohabitation agreement had been treated more like a business arrangement, complete with contracts and obligations and consequences for failing to meet them, I'd have been in a much better place than I found myself in after Dick moved out.

So let's start with...

Resolution: Many modern acts have sections encouraging parties to try to resolve separation issues outside of court. We've all watched a lot of TV shows where the gallant lawyer or the savvy judge finally triumphs over evil and saves your day. But the reality is that no one really wants to hear your case in court. Court is expensive and judges are very busy trying cases where people have been irreparably injured and we're just brokenhearted with a massive mortgage and diminished bank account. Therefore, if you're like me, you will get all kinds of pressure to settle through negotiation, mediation, or arbitration, including from your own lawyer. If you don't jump through these hoops, the judge won't like you, the lawyers say, so you have to go through these steps. And these steps all cost lots and lots of money.

Parentage and parenting: This section of family law determines who is a parent and what responsibilities they have to the children produced by, or involved in, the union. Dicey stuff these days, what with step parenting and turkey basters. How do you define a parent in the twenty-first century, or a family for that matter? Kudos to the *FLA* for giving it a shot, and even bigger high-fives for making sure that kids from non-traditional unions get a fair shake.

Property division: This stipulates what is family property and what is excluded property, and how both are divided. If you are a person with some assets like a house or retirement savings and you're in a relationship with someone who doesn't have these things, you're not going to like this section very much. This includes property assessment and appraisals and at what point after you've split with your partner do you calculate who gets what. You won't like that part either.

Pension division: This section describes what pension benefits are divisible and by how much. Like property division, if you're someone who works hard and saves through a pension program, and you're in a relationship with someone who does neither, this section will also suck for you. It can be one of the more shockingly unfair sections in BC's *Family Law Act*, not in principle – which is to protect a stay-at-home parent - but in actuality, when the other party simply doesn't want to work or save, but still gets half.

Spousal support: This part deals with the conditions under which a spouse is entitled to receive support payments from the other. Some of it certainly sounds fair, and apparently these days the courts are trying to encourage both parties to become self-sufficient as quickly as possible, but that could still mean years of dividing your salary and the law doesn't care about partners who decide not to work because their Wendys (or Wendells) are all too willing to support them. And it has nothing to say about the partner who pursued their dream of becoming a world-famous screenwriter and hung about on la Croissette jonesing for Spielberg's phone number instead of going home to make some money to help pay the bills... Oh whoops, that was me.

On the other hand, I know of someone who gave up a good job to move across the country with his new wife to support her high-powered career and to become the primary caregiver to her kids from another relationship. Now that the children are grown, he and his wife are splitting up, and his career has been stalled for years. Should he get some support from his ex? This is the kind of spouse family law can protect, as long as he hasn't signed a cohab that gave away this entitlement.

Child support: I'm not going into this part too much since Dick and I didn't have kids together, so I don't have any experience with this. But I believe if someone has kids, they are responsible for their ongoing care and well-being, no matter what happens to their relationship. If they don't take that responsibility, they are a supreme derelict asshole, and that's pretty much all I have to say about that. Unless the children are from a previous relationship, like the friend I mentioned earlier. This a situation with nuance, where the lines between legal and moral responsibility can get blurry[50] I know someone with a very high-demand, high-salary job married someone with a child who turned out to have a severe mental health problem that eventually drove the couple apart. Had she been told that going in, what would her choices have been? What should they be now?

Regardless of your situation, please review the federal guidelines to understand your rights and responsibilities regarding child support, which cannot be waived, in Canada[51] or in the United States.[52]

Abuse and family violence: Abuse is a broad term and violence is a criminal matter, not a civil one. Not all jurisdictions go here: even though BC's *FLA* does attempt to navigate these troubling waters, it does not protect the assets of someone who has been abused in their relationship. Whatever Dick did to me financially and emotionally, it doesn't compare to what some people are subjected to at the hands of their partners, where relying on a cohab agreement to protect you is like trying to fend off a bear with a blade of grass. The only way to protect yourself is to imagine the unthinkable right from the beginning. And if you're doing that, then *you might just want to avoid the relationship altogether!* Because once you're in it, it's too late and the *FLA* doesn't have the instruments to help you. That family violence has happened so many times in the past in so many different cultures, and continues to happen to this day, that more than half of the women murdered are killed by their romantic partner,[53] this is an incomprehensible horror for which I have no words, no experience, and certainly no advice.[54] That family law, at least in some jurisdictions, has to intersect with what is a crime, pure and simple, gives us a taste of the contradictions and insanity inherent in the state attempting to govern human relationships.

The rest of the *FLA* is about court procedures, when to file what document, what form to use and when, what you can and can't do in court, enforcement of orders, appeals, and so on. The hope is, with the right agreement in place, none of that should be necessary. (Unless you're a victim of domestic violence. Or seeking support for children unforeseen at the time the cohab was drafted. If those are your circumstances, please go to the police, or get some professional assistance, seek all the help the law can offer you.)

Because here's the other thing: some people lie. Especially the narcissistic ones. Not only do they lie to us, they lie to themselves, creating their own mythology, their own alternate reality that has nothing to do with ours. Dick denied his promises and the agreements we had made and that he had breached. The most pointed one was the romantic promise to never take a dime from me - completely denied he ever said that, that the infamous date on which he made that promise even happened. Dick was quite adept at drawing a person into tales of woe and persecution and he aimed to convince the judge, with moist blue eyes and trembling lips, that he deserved every penny he was asking for. In his mind, the money was already his! Because *this was his reality,* and what he was going to say in court. And he was so convincing—calm, smooth, charming

—that the lawyers soon decided he was more persuasive than an angry, anxiety-ridden, cry-baby screaming that she'd been strung along, used, abused, and scorned before she was tossed aside. Who could blame this poor man for running for all he was worth from such a bag, Your Honour, I ask you?!

Dick had fooled me for years, and now he was going to fool the judge as well.

"Falsehood flies, and the truth comes limping after it."
—Jonathan Swift

Here's what I learned about the Law: it likes to split things down the middle, no questions asked, unless you have an agreement that says otherwise

What you can do: write a cohab that represents your boundaries, and the outcomes from a breakup that you can live with

CHAPTER 9: SHEEP-DIPPED BY CONTRACT

I mentioned that we often fall out of love with someone for the same reasons we fall in love with them. And in my experience with Dick, that is absolutely true. He was impulsive, adventurous, philosophical, and lived for the moment – all the things a Wendy isn't. It was the twenty-something romance I had missed because I got married so young to a man who made me feel safe rather than truly alive. What I failed to realize is that you do all those lovely things with someone like Dick for a while, but you don't, to borrow from Beyoncé, try to put a ring on it. Because marriage, real commitment, keeping up a home together, child-care, maintaining responsibilities like full-time work and paying a mortgage: those are things the Peter Pans of the world cannot do. And when you try to make them, they start to hate you. And when someone you love hates you, you start to hate yourself.

But it takes two to Zumba around the Roomba, so we may ask ourselves: *What were my contributions to this disaster? And why did this happen to me?*

People come into our lives for a reason and they leave for an even more important one. And, supposedly, the more painful the end of the relationship, the more valuable the. I mentioned my guilt over my previous relationship ending and that pursuing my dream of becoming a writer put me in a position of financial dependence, which ended up in me feeling like a bum benefiting from family law when that relationship ended. Oh, come on, I'm pretty sure I did, at least once! So, one could say – and actually my mom did say – that Dick was my comeuppance, my karma, the man I chose to balance my deadbeat-ism with his own. How terrifying if that's the way the world actually works!

The VBP I worked with told me that people often seek out partners for the second (aka adult) family who in some way mirrors the wounds and insufficiencies of our first (aka childhood) family. I know my mother loved me, but she had a hard time expressing it in healthy, affirming ways because of her own trauma. As a result, I grew up feeling judged, unloved, and unsafe. So, guess what, I married a man who made me feel safe, for a while, until he started to judge me for not meeting his standards. And then I turned around and (trauma) bonded with someone who made me feel unjudged (at first, anyway) but unsafe.

The upshot of all this was one very stressed-out, anxious lady desperately trying to make a relationship work with a scamp, and the one thing I would actually apologize to Dick for was how horribly needy I could be at times. Because what I really needed to do before getting involved with any of these men was to learn to love myself more than anyone else, and to accept (i.e., not judge) myself for who I truly was - as opposed to some image or set of standards, or ability to procreate, or set of bank accounts. If I'd done that, I probably would not have married my first husband and Dick would never have stood a chance.

[#]

Dick's lawyer kept saying that our cohab agreement was clear that I owed him lots and lots of money out of the house and half my pension. Plain and simple, no strings attached. Frustrated with this interpretation, I went back to the legal firm who had drafted the cohab in the first place. Lawyers No. 1 and No. 2 were both gone by this point, and Lawyer No. 5 had replaced Lawyer No. 2, who had replaced Lawyer No. 1. Ya, I'm a bit dizzy too but stick with me here because Lawyer No. 5 is now telling me that the connection between Dick's contributions and him getting a chunk of the house was *implicit*. Oh, so... I'm fine? Really? That's great! The thousands of dollars I paid your firm to protect me really was worth it? Hurrah! I'm still heartbroken, but not broke! Yay, me!

Not so fast, said Dick's lawyer. Nowhere in this cohab did it *explicitly* say: Dick has to contribute this much every month or he doesn't get. Nowhere does it say: Dick has to retain pensionable employment or he isn't entitled to any of your pension. I mean, it made perfect sense to me at the time... you contribute, you reap the benefits of that contribution. That's the way the world works, right? Why does it have to be explicitly stated?

Because, many a lawyer would eventually tell me, if it's not perfectly clear that the intent was, you're asking the judge to make an interpretation, and that judge could very well interpret it as Dick and his lawyer were – that no matter what we'd promised each other, no matter what the situation was when we signed the agreement – he gets hundreds of thousands of dollars. That's what your contract actually says, Lawyer No. 4 warned me. Another freakout moment for me, this time vented at my lawyer (sorry, No. 4).

"Why would you do that?" Lawyer No. 6 had asked me, incredulously, "that's crazy." Yes, I had gone to yet another lawyer for yet another opinion, hers being that I must've been temporarily insane and was now permanently hooped. According to Westlaw Canada:

> *"A contract is a legally recognized agreement between two or more persons which gives rise to an obligation that may be enforced in the courts. More comprehensively, a valid and operative contract may be defined as an agreement free from vitiating factors such as mistake or misrepresentation, and constituted by the unconditional acceptance of an outstanding offer involving a reasonably precise and complete set of terms between two or more contractually competent parties..."*[55]

But, but, but, I kept telling all these lawyers, I entered into an agreement full of vitiating factors! Where I was lied to and manipulated into agreeing to fleece myself! Can't I get out of it?

"A contract is a contract is a contract," Lawyer No. 7 tells me. It's now several months after Dick and I had broken up. No. 7 was talking about the amended agreement we had made later in our relationship, one that allowed me to keep more of my house in the event of a breakup, which he was now denying ever existed. This lawyer, a civil litigator, was encouraging me to pursue my efforts to split assets under the second agreement, even though Dick never signed it. But what she was telling me is true for any contract, especially for a signed one where both parties had legal representation, which was the case for the first cohab, which was now sucking a lot for me.

What constitutes a contract? Offer and acceptance, essentially, and the absence of duress. Duress can range from signing something because someone has a gun to your head to signing something because you didn't understand it. But I'd had the advice of two lawyers drafting that agreement. Gaslit like an oil refinery on fire, I offered Dick a contract where he was entitled to half a million dollars out of my house plus half my pension, he accepted it, both parties signed through legal counsel. Done and dusted.

Meanwhile, agreements to agree, which is what Dick was saying our second agreement was, are not enforceable:

> "Even when parties intend to contract, the essential terms of the bargain must be agreed and possess a sufficient degree of clarity before a legally binding agreement can be said to exist. Where, therefore, an agreement is incomplete because essential provisions have not been settled, or the agreement is too general or uncertain to be valid in itself, or the understanding of the parties is that their legal obligations are to be deferred until a formal contract has been executed, no binding contract will have been created..."[56]

In plain English, I was flocked.

All this is to say that once we've been masterfully manipulated into crossing our own boundaries to the point we actually instruct our lawyer to write an agreement that doesn't serve us, the courts will uphold it. Being a victim of gaslighting is not a legal argument.

Here's what I learned about the Law: it is precise and explicit, and allows judges to uphold valid contracts.

What you can do: Don't let anyone—especially someone who says they love you—manipulate you into a trap where you stew your own lamb.

CHAPTER 10: PARTIALLY FLOCKED

Grief and anger can be the flip sides of the same record, just like love and hate. So sometimes I wondered, was I holding out on Dick's demands for money because I'm mad, sad, or both? Was I sad? Of course, I was. Incredibly, agonizingly, ridiculously sad. I thought I had lost my last chance at true love, lost the dream of riding off into the sunset with my Lost Boy-Prince Charming, whom I had rescued from his Lonely Lostness and who had rescued me from my Lonely Princess-ness. Cue the credits and fun-cute cartoons over a top-ten hit song!

Dick was a fantasy and I loved the fantasy more than the man, and now I realize that's what I was truly grieving – the loss of that romantic fairytale. That I'd one day meet the "One" who would make dreams, adventure, and never-ending love come true. The Neverland Dick promised but couldn't actually deliver. I got caught up in the crossfire of his lack of self-worth and his quest to be the superhero of childish fantasies, and he got caught up in mine.

How terribly sad…

Sidebar Your Honour – sometimes people fight so hard with their exes, not for a fair deal, but because they can't let them go. While there's a fight there's still *some kind* of relationship, even if just a sad and icky one.

Objection! We had agreements! I'm fighting for what we agreed to! He didn't want to work! He didn't want to contribute! And yet... part of me wondered...

Was that what I was doing? Was I really fighting for what's fair? Or was I trying to hold on to my fairytale? And the horrible possibility that I (gasp) could spend the rest of my life alone, as a single woman (horror of horrors!)? Other times, I would just beat myself up for being all the things Dick said I was – controlling, jealous, and, of course, petty.

Full of self doubt, I would often falter, especially after what Lawyers No. 4 and No. 6 had to say. But I had wonderful support from friends and family. Especially my dad, who was terribly ill at the time but still found the strength to encourage me to do what I believed was right. Just like he always did. Plus, damn! If I gave Dick what he wanted I could be homeless and working until I was eighty to pay off my debts and recover my savings. But I admit, mostly what kept me going was my fury over being scammed.

And when you're that mad, here's what happens next...

The Letter Missiles

Lawyers are paid to do what you want, as long as it's within the confines of the law (I'm talking about *most* lawyers, okay, not some of the ones in the news). So once I told mine that I wanted to fight, he squared off with Dick's lawyer like roosters in a cockfight. The first weapon fired: the letters. Thinly veiled threats designed to make Dick and me feel quite chuffed with ourselves, not to mention vindicated. These letters really were works of art, complete with theatrics (*how dare she deny his entitlement to... how could he possibly think he was entitled to...*) and clever twists of phrase (*in what world does such larceny not induce punishment rather than reward!*). How wonderful to read such a thing when you've been feeling so flocked over for so long!

But the more aggressive, the more threatening, the more likely this letter-firing is being used to appease a client who is full of rage and frothing at the mouth. And, I'm embarrassed to admit, a lot of times that mouth-frother was me. There was something so satisfying about an eloquent lawyer serving Dick the words I'd never had the ability to dish out myself. But, alas, as satisfying as it was, telling someone to self-fornicate while leaping from a tall structure without a parachute generally speaking doesn't convince them to see your point of view. Plus, it costs a lot of money!

Thus the next letter from Dick's side threatened a trial and a lien on my house if I didn't pay up. Dick wanted to get on with his life which involved buying property with his new lady-love and my money. No shock that the next letter from my lawyer basically said F.O.A.D., you fraudulent, usurious, abusive piece of shit.

Apparently them's fightin' words, because next came the...

Family Claim & Pleadings

The first step after someone files for a family law claim is what is called "the initial pleadings". Basically, this is asking for a trial as a family law action. Dick's lawyer filed a document at the Supreme Court called a *pleading*, which in my case was Dick pleading to the court to make me give him lots and lots of money. Often the pleadings will reference different sections of the legal act to justify why Dick should get all this money for this and that reason. Then my lawyer has to send a response saying, No, Dick should *not* get all this money for this and that reason. This is also a pleading, which is also called a *counterclaim*. So now Dick is the claimant in a family law action, and I am the respondent, which basically means Dick says, "I claim all this money because it is mine under the this and that section of the *Family Law Act*," and my response is, "Go to hell," or something like that but in legalese so it sounds better.

Guns drawn at dawn and the sheep are scared. But they shouldn't be because this was still a lot of smoke and mirrors for the frother's benefit. It's all designed to get one of us— the least stubborn, the most empathetic one, the one who can't afford trial, or the one who just wants to get on with their life —to cave. But Dick didn't walk away—he'd invested seven years on this payout and he was going to get it, no matter what. And I didn't cave—I'd wasted seven years of my life with someone who pretended to love me so they could sponge off me, and I wasn't going to pay him for the privilege.

The saying goes that the only ones who benefit from a

legal conflict are the lawyers—and that would seem, based on my experience, correct. So, with neither of us backing down in the face of letter missiles and threats of trial, next came...

Financial Disclosure

This is where separating couples share financial information with each other in order to determine property, debt, and pension divisions as well as child and spousal support. A dry and painful process of filling out forms that lawyers provide and guide, particularly painful for someone like me, who's assets had grown substantially over the course of the relationship, no thanks to Dick.

My house had increased in value and now I had to pay an official appraiser to tell Dick and his shark by exactly how much. You guessed it – it had more than doubled in value. Under the old cohab, I would lose it in order to pay Dick what he was demanding. Under the FLA, no question, my house was a goner, along with my savings and half my pension as well. Even better, I'd be shocked to learn, said pension had grown too... by a lot, increasing the money I owed Dick under the FLA and the old cohab.

How could that even be? To my mind, 1) my pension had been non-existent when Dick and I signed the first agreement, 2) Dick had nothing to do with me getting and maintaining pensionable employ, 3) I only agreed to split because he had, at the time, a pension he was going to split with me! How could I now owe him all of this other money as well!?

Yay me, more painful lessons!

I'll get into how tricky pension and evaluation and division can be later, but right now, Dick's lawyer (aka the shark) is saying that if we don't settle quickly on the basis of the original cohab, Dick's going for the full-meal deal under the FLA. That means half of everything and spousal support to boot. Holy Cowboy Boots! Which means that one of us was feeling very entitled to lots and lots of money and the other (me!) was feeling horribly flocked over.

At this point, after reviewing all the financials, asset evaluations, income, and the shark's most recent threat, my lawyer suggests I up my offer to Dick substantially. Because if this did go to trial and the judge overturned the original cohab, I'd get flocked even worse. I know I'm supposed to feel scared but instead I start to wonder if I need a new lawyer. For now, I just say, hell no and fuck that. Which means the next thing on the menu is the...

Case Conferences

In BC, this is called a judicial *case conference*, or a JCC. Basically, it's a meeting where I, Dick, our lawyers, and a judge sit down together so the judge can try to convince me to mediate and settle out of court. The Shark said all kinds of unflattering things about me (*she told him he didn't deserve a dime, your Honour, after all he's done for her*), trying to convince the judge to say, *Well now, if that's the case, Wendy's in a lot of trouble! How dare she not give poor Dick all this money! What an unreasonable, spiteful wretch, and poor, sweet Dick!*

My lawyer basically said nothing, allowing Dick to feel

righteous and sanctified and me to feel desperate and hopeless. Another terrible flocking, which cost me a few thousand dollars. In hindsight, I suspect that the strategy to get me to surrender started then, two years before the case got even close to settling. If I were really cynical, I might even suspect the lawyers worked out a strategy between them. *You do this and this, and I'll say this and that, and then she'll have to…. And then he'll have no choice but to…* Does that happen? I have no idea.

In BC Supreme Court cases, and in some other jurisdictions, there are also *trial management conferences*, or TMCs. These are designed to get everyone prepped for trial, where the lawyers go before a judge, present a summary of the conflict, the witnesses if any, and any number of documents to cover so that the judge can decide whether or not the number of trial days assigned will be enough. If it's not, the judge may decide to adjourn until you can get a longer trial. But it's also another opportunity for the judge to encourage the lawyers to get the parties to settle. And that pressure on the lawyers translated to pressure on me, once again, to roll over. Which I didn't. But the longer I held out, the bigger that pressure got.

I started to get an inkling feeling of this during the JCC, when the judge was swayed by the shark's characterization of the situation and seemed completely unaware of the fact that I was trying to settle under the amended agreement Dick and I had agreed upon - uh, helloooo, No. 4 - and so I was already pretty upset when the judge suggested mediation. Mediation? How the hell does that work when one of you is either a con artist or a total flake?!

I must've said that last bit out loud because the outcome

of the JCC was setting a trial date in two months. Not a lot of time! No problem, I told myself, completely convinced I'd get Judge Judy who would see Dick for the dick he was and finally give us both the justice we deserved. However, real life has a way of getting in the way of these things which means that more often than not, there will be an...

Adjournment

This is either a postponement, or a suspension, of an appearance at court or any other legal proceeding. Once a court date is scheduled, either party can ask for an adjournment at any time for any reason, and if both parties agree to the delay, the trial will be postponed. There are all kinds of reasons - some good, some not so good[57]- to adjourn trial, from not having enough money to pay the lawyer, to family illness, to a serious work commitment, and, last but not least... adjourning to go to...

Mediation

Dick really didn't want to go to trial and kept pressing for mediation. But I didn't want to mediate. What's the point in negotiating with a narcissistic phoney, I said to the judge at the JCC and to No. 4 every time he brought it up.

"Collaborative law is a bunch of bunk," Lawyer No. 8, a very senior, nearly-retired lawyer that a friend recommended I speak to. Judges like it because it's quicker and cheaper than court, she told me, but it just doesn't work in high-conflict cases. So if you have been abused in any way during your relationship, don't waste your time, hopes, and money on it – was the gist of her advice.

Feeling abused by Dick's false promises and gaslighting, I felt convinced that mine was one of those cases No.8 was referring to. But, when No. 4 and I had to go back to Dick and his shark, hat in hand, asking for an adjournment so I could attend to a work commitment - so I could keep the job that allowed me to keep up the mortgage payments Dick was not contributing to - the response was sure, but only if you agree to the mediation you so thoroughly poo-pooed during the JCC. Argh! Another sheep-dipped moment for me, but at this point I had no choice.

[#]

At first, it wasn't so bad. The mediator prepped me by asking what I hoped to achieve and I said "to tell Dick to plunge head first into a lava pool for breaking my heart and scamming me!" Okay, I agree, that's an unlikely outcome. So instead I said, "I want us to settle under the amending agreement like we agreed when we reconciled a few years ago." And he seemed to think that was reasonable. Yay me!

But during actual mediation both Dick and I were too firmly entrenched in our positions and on the promises of the other person. I suppose in Dick's mind, I'd reneged on my promise to give him lots and lots of money if (when) he ever left. So, all mediation ended up being was basically me and my lawyer holding down our fort and supporting our position, and Dick and his lawyer doing the same, with the mediator bouncing back and forth between us delivering messages and threats. Essentially, the letter missiles again, but in human form this time. And a stupid waste of money, especially when one of you feels extremely entitled and the other feels horribly flocked over. Not to mention manipulated. I think the real reason Dick wanted me in mediation was so that someone else, other than his shark and the JCC judge, could threaten me with eternal damnation and poverty if I didn't pay him what he wanted.

So, no shock, nothing was achieved, but that will be another $6,000 dollars please.

Now What?

If I was angry before, there are no words to describe how I felt now. I pulled out all the stops, even going as far as to consult with another civil litigator (this was No. 9 now) about whether I could sue Dick for breach of contract and fraud in civil court, if my bid to uphold the amendment in family law court failed. My thinking was not without precedent. When the criminal trial against O.J. Simpson failed, the families of the people he was accused of murdering sued him in civil court. And won[58].

"Sorry," Lawyer No. 9 tells me, "You're under the purview of family law, and it's going to stay in family law, no matter what happens.

"That sucks," I said, or something close to that.

"Ya, especially since family law favours deadbeats."

O where were you, lo these many years ago, when I was drafting my cohab with Dick, I wanted to ask No. 9. But instead I ask, "What about the people who work hard, save their money, and grow their assets?"

"They're fucked."

What a succinct summary of my relationship with Dick and current situation.

Here's what I learned about the Law: in a legal framework that favours deadbeats, your lawyer can't really protect you.

Here's what I learned about Love: in this kind of scenario, no one can be as cruel as someone who once said they love you.

What you can do: aside from the obvious - don't fall in love with a deadbeat - write an unflockably explicit cohab agreement.

CHAPTER 11:
UDDERLY FLOCKED

Okay. So. Here we are.

I didn't have an unflockable cohab, but decided to fight anyway. I got pounded at the JCC because I have a collaborative lawyer while Dick has a shark. The mediator was basically an overpaid messenger who just kept trying to scare me with visions of doom and bankruptcy unless I rolled and gave Dick what he wanted. I felt bruised, sore, punched in the gut and down for the count. But a quick chat with my dad made me realize I wasn't ready for the ropes. I rallied! Despite many sweaty, sleepless nights and developing a nervous tick and a terrible wine-and-chips habit, I was able to jump up and head back into the fray, ready for more flocking!

What's next? Ah, *discovery*!!

Not as much fun as it sounds...

Examinations For Discovery

Now that I've spent tons of money exchanging frothy letters, claims, counterclaims, amended claims, financial statements, tax returns, property assessments, JCCs, and fruitless mediation, the next stop on my one-way ticket to family law court is the *examination for discovery.*

This is a meeting where "one party asks an opposing party questions about the issues in the dispute" which are part of the litigation process but take place outside of court and without judges.[59] This means my lawyer gets to grill Dick over every broken promise, every abuse, and I get to watch. Sounds pretty good, right? I couldn't wait to watch my lawyer tear Dick a new bodily orifice over his betrayal and his lies. Laying bare for all to see his true nature and the vast scope of his depravity, leaving him a sobbing, puddled mess full of despair and contrition. Hurrah! Yay me!

True, Dick's shark would get a chance to do the same to me, but who cares! In fact, I welcomed the chance to have my say because I, unlike Dick, am telling the truth! I may be bruised and thousands of dollars in the hole but it would be worth it, just for this! Because now, all of us, lawyers and all, will see what a victim I was and what a true deadbeat Dick was and then I. Shall. Finally. Be. AVENGED!

Not so fast...

Discovery isn't really about digging out the truth, at least not in my experience. It's about whose story is going to sound better in court. Sure, your lawyer will try to verify some facts and get your ex (or you) to admit some stuff, but it's more about who's going to be the more credible witness. Well, guess what? It wasn't going to be me.

People like my ex tend to be pretty good at this stuff

because they believe their own lies, their own version of reality, so deeply, they make others believe it too. Remember, that's how we got into this mess in the first place. Right? Because they are smooth, quiet, consistent, and quite charming. While we, Wendy (or Wendell), are trying so hard to stick to the truth and be brutally honest and transparent that we end up looking like babbling idiots.

> *"Honesty has no defence against superior cunning."*—*Gulliver's Travels*, Jonathan Swift, 1726 (1726?! And still relevant. Very cool.)

I thought I had reams of proof, documents, spreadsheets, and a good grasp of the chronology of events and couldn't wait to share it with Dick and his shark. But sometimes, too much information can be a bad thing. My lawyer should have told me to KISS it (keep it simple stupid) but he didn't. And so I babbled away during my discovery, referring to this and that spreadsheet, and this and that event, giving the shark plenty of opportunities to twist me and my story around so many times that I got emotional and confused and looked like a complete moron to everyone including the court reporter. I was so embarrassed, desperately wishing I could take back a bunch of stuff that I said, or clarify what I said, except now it's part of the court record and I've spent another $5,000 or so convincing my own lawyer that I'll do terribly on the stand. While Dick and his shark get to go on believing his simple, slickly-told version of the story.

Hmmm. Perhaps at this point, Wendy/Wendell, you are thinking that this "fighting the system along with your ex" is starting to look like a really bad idea. Well, don't worry. It gets worse.

Costs

At one point a friend asked me, "Do you have to pay for his legal fees?" The simple answer is no, each party has to pay for their own lawyer in family law. Some jurisdictions offer free legal aid to those who can't afford it, but most disallow lawyers to be paid on contingency (i.e., getting a cut of the deal) the way they do in accident cases or a class-action lawsuit against a corporation. In family law, you have to pay the fees straight up so there is no incentive for claimants or lawyers to go after more than their *FLA* entitles them to.

What often happens, though, is the claimant (i.e., Dick, in this case) doesn't have to pay until after he gets the money, and the lawyer arranges with their client that they will get paid out of the settlement in the consent order. Lawyers will often do this when they are sure their fees will be covered by the amount their client is getting. Meanwhile, the respondent (i.e., me, in this case) has to pay their lawyer upfront. It's a bit unfair in my view because the process in this situation is relatively pain-free for the claimant, like a credit card, buy now, pay later, and can lead to "bingeing" on legal fees they may otherwise avoid. Dick was quite quick to file court application after court application whenever he didn't get his way, or felt I was dragging my feet (of course I was!), which must have cost a few thousand dollars in additional fees.

However, as the case went on, Dick's shark made applications for me to pay Dick's legal fees, because I wouldn't settle. Regular costs are like a tariff, much less than the legal and documentation costs, but it's still unpleasant when you have to pay them. In only one application was Dick able to get some costs awarded, a few hundred dollars, when I asked for an adjournment to get a new lawyer up to speed. However, in some cases, where the judge decides a party's actions are particularly egregious, they may award "special costs," which can be tantamount to you paying for your ex's lawyer. Of course, that's to be avoided, but you'd have to have done something really naughty, like puncturing your ex's tires so they couldn't get to court on time or calling in a bomb threat just before the application is about to be heard (not to give you any ideas!). Nevertheless, the lawyers, and in a couple of case conferences, the judges as well, threatened me with "costs being awarded against you," in another bid to encourage me to settle out of court. Again and again, I had to decide how strong I thought my case was, and whether or not my lawyer still believed in it. And in me...

Prepping For Trial

"You need a new lawyer," my dad yelled at me, not for the first time. He was angry when I told him about the lack of prep before my discovery, but he'd gone sour on No. 4 since the JCC.

"But, but, but," I stuttered back, full of excuses... it's too close to trial, he's done so much for me, I really think he knows what he's doing, his firm has a great reputation..." until even I could hear the echoes from my defending Dick during our relationship. I'd like to think I'm just loyal to a fault but probably it's just fear. Either way, this would be another time I wish I'd made a change sooner.

I did consult with another lawyer though. Enter Lawyer No. 10. A seasoned attorney with a reputation of being a barracuda. She was retiring soon and so refused to take my case (or maybe she knew something I didn't) but as a friend of a friend, she agreed to consult with me as a "shadow" lawyer, a second pair of expert eyes on how my case was unfolding and how my lawyer was handling things. She also gave me great advice on ways to push back on what was happening to me.

I took a few of these ideas to Lawyer No. 4 and in the weeks leading to trial, he amended our counterclaim to ask the court to uphold the amended agreement on the basis of a section buried in the FLA on *unwritten or unsigned agreements* between the parties, provided they could be proven, in order to avoid Dick being *unjustly enriched* at my expense. Yay me!

Dick and his shark fought back with a demand to have my house re-evaluated. In the intervening year or so since we split, my house shot up in value again! It was now worth almost three times what I paid for it and because I called the original cohab into question – which stipulated the value of the house be divided *at separation* – Dick could now claim division as of *at trial*, even though I was the only one (still) paying all its expenses. Once again, I was completely floored by how unfair family law can be because now he wanted half of what my house was worth today, plus half my pension, which had also gone up again, plus spousal support. I would be living in my mother's basement for eternity, working until I was 100, and pimping out my horse for pony rides at the park.

The thing was, no one really wanted to go to trial. Except for me. Yes, I was just that insa... no, wait - persistent, yes, that's what we're going with - because I felt that, properly prepped, I had enough evidence to convince the judge to settle the case on the basis of the unsigned agreement in order to avoid Dick's unjust enrichment. But I was the only one who wanted to go through with it, my lawyer included, who had started humming the famous song from Disney's *Frozen*[60] during our meetings. Which, having watched too many episodes of *Law & Order* where fairness wins the day, baffled me.

Everyone was finding reasons to postpone the day Dick and I had to stand up in front of a judge. Here are a few that I experienced:

"I have a work commitment that I can't get out of" (that was me).

"I fainted and got a doctor's note" (one of our lawyers).

"My mother is in the hospital" (me again, totally true!).

"We need adjourn so we can get the house re-evaluated, another mediation, another discovery, because I'm on vacation, etc". (both lawyers, more than once)

More and more it seemed to me that the spectre of *trial* —where a *judge* looks down upon us and metes out some semblance of justice based on their reading of the law and two competing versions of truth, a judge who may be in a bad mood, impatient, or simply have experience and opinions that are wildly different from yours or your lawyer's, and who might be the judge your lawyer has to face another day— was just too much poker.

Speaking of which, how much of this was bluffing? Win or lose, trial is an expensive risk, and all of us were trying hard to find a reason to put it off, kick that stinky can on down the road, in the hopes that something will eventually come up to avoid it altogether. Like Wendy finally accepting that it's simply her fate to be fleeced and settle up.

Most of the time, No. 10 told me, trial will be adjourned, at least a few times. But even if you do get your ass dragged to court, don't let your ex spook you into something that is grossly unfair. Because, she said, if you think about it, there are only a few possible outcomes:

> Your ex will say, "Okay, okay, let's adjourn and negotiate a little more."
> The judge will say, "Wendy/Wendell, I agree with you. Your ex is a deadbeat and shouldn't get a dime."
> The judge will say, "Dick/Dickette, I agree with you. Wendy/Wendell is a stingy shit who owes you their house, a kidney, and their sister's next born."
> The judge will say, "Wendy/Wendell, Dick/Dickette, you're both pricks and this is a bunch of BS at taxpayer expense so I'm splitting it down the middle."

Which one of the above is the most likely to happen? That's the gamble, the *big question* I had to ask myself before deciding to go—or not—to trial on the pre-ordained, much-dreaded, and quite possibly to be adjourned, day. Most of the time, No. 10 said, unless you can prove that you both agreed otherwise, it's door No. 4.

At this point I was reeling with doubt. How strong was

my case, really? How likely is it that the judge will slice and dice according to the FLA, or the original cohab? How likely is it that I'll have to pay spousal support? Am I really just dragging Dick to court because I'm so pissed off that I got hornswoggled? Or do I actually have a case supported by the law? I wasn't sure how much I trusted No. 4 anymore so I turned up the mike on my gut and asked it if I had a cold hope in hell, and it said...

"Don't quit now."

Ok, maybe that was my dad. The point is I'd gathered enough legal advice by now to feel pretty sure that Dick wouldn't qualify for spousal support (good luck with that, Lawyer No. 6 had said) but other than that, I was taking a pretty big risk. Because no one really knows for sure how a case will be handled by a judge in a system that favours deadbeats. And that's why my lawyer, when we were supposed to be prepping for trial, started maneuvering me towards making one last Ave Maria attempt to settle. An offer made on the eve of trial, when I was a nervous, jangly wreck and pretty close to the lowest point in my life.

Because my dad was really sick at this point. I went to see him at the hospital and the only thing that made him smile was me telling him that I was still swinging (but just barely).

So back to No. 4's office for what I thought would be me practising my testimony and No. 4 figuring out what and how to ask the questions that would prove my case. Instead, I found myself embroiled in negotiations with Dick again, being told by my own lawyer that I had to "let it go" when it came to my pension.

When things got really crunchy – basically me starting to

cry, begging for my day in court – the senior partner (this was Lawyer No. 3 again) strolled in to tell me a horrifying truth. He had recently represented a woman in court who had bought her own house but married some cretin who beat her. She left him for that reason and he sued her for half the house. The senior partner, with twenty-five years of experience in family law, could not convince a judge that this bottom-dweller didn't deserve his millions from the house he had nothing to do with aside from living in it while beating the crap out of its owner. There is no instrument in family law that prevents this nauseating outcome. She could press charges in criminal court, but that didn't help her save her house, even if her abuser went to jail. So, what hope did I have, convincing a judge not to give Dick his half a mil, when all he did is con me and inflict a little emotional abuse along the way? Not very much.

So that's how No. 4 got me to agree to give a settlement one last go, on a Friday, when our trial was on Monday and he was going away for the weekend. Which meant I had to decide now. A typical scenario, apparently, which I didn't realize until too late, and here's how it works.

The Pre-Trial Offer (Aka Boil The Frog)

With the clock ticking loudly towards doomsday, when I had to face the bogeyman (or bogeywoman) judge, No. 4 says let's make an offer that is both something "you can live with" and reasonably close to what we think the judge is going to do.

Okay, okay, I said. I was tired, stretched to the bone on the rack of legal bills, I wanted to spend more time with my dad, so

I said - let's split the difference between what the cohab says he gets and what the amendment says he gets. No pension division, though, because that's just ridiculous. There you go, Shark! I thought. Take it or leave it, Dick! Because, No. 4 told me, if we've made a reasonable offer and the judge agrees with us, and says that Dick should have accepted the offer, then Dick has to pay *me* costs! Plus, I've saved the $50k or so it would have cost to go to court. Hurrah! Yay me!

Not so fast, says Dick's shark. The cohab says you owe him half your pension, period. It doesn't say you only owe him if he contributes to a pension too.

Wait, yes it does! Well, it kind of does... I only agreed to split my pension because he had a pension that he was going to split! But he quit that job and cashed in that pension so no deal... right?

That's not what your deal actually says, said the shark. So, we'll take your offer of the house split, AND half your pension, and you have to say yes to this offer by midnight tonight or we're going to charge you an additional $5,000 for every hour that you delay.

What? What kind of dick would do this? I met him halfway! He knew both my parents were ill! Frantic, I tried calling No. 4 – what do I do??? But he was on his weekend vacation and hard to reach. No. 10 wasn't available either. And while I was waiting to talk to No. 4, the shark added another $5,000 to what she said I had to pay Dick.

Oh, flock me.

Here's what I learned about the Law: you and your lawyer have to be on the same page, every step of the way, or you'll get seriously flocked

Here's what I learned about Love: the breakup will be as painful, and as costly, as the relationship

What you can do: at this stage, not very much.

CHAPTER 12: BUT STILL KICKING

I finally did get a hold of No. 4, and he was able to convince the shark to drop the extra $5k but only if I said yes to the deal right now. To be fair to No. 4, he felt he'd done his due diligence, going back and forth with me and Dick for hours, checking in with more senior partners, including No. 3 – is this a fair deal? And they all told him to tell me to jump at it. So, after guzzling half a bottle of Pinot Noir – a very good one too because after this I'd be drinking plonk – I finally caved… sort of.

In the morning, I woke up with one of those WHAT THE HELL DID I JUST DO moments. Yes, okay, maybe you're hearing an echo of my relationship with Dick, but you can't tell these things at the time, especially when one is recovering from drinking too much Pinot! I called No. 10 in a panic, who told me I should never have paid attention to the threats of additional money added on to the offer.

That's a total tactic… your lawyer didn't tell you that? And what about making sure you understood everything, including the ramifications of splitting your pension. What about making sure the lien on your house was removed, was that in there? At this stage in the game, you and your lawyer have to go over every line, make sure it's all there, all the conditions, that you agree with every single last thing, before you say yes... didn't your lawyer do that?

No, no, and no.

I fired No. 4.

"Finally!" whooped my dad. Well, it was more of a rasp. He was home from the hospital now but was very weak. "Now go get somebody who's gonna fight for you."

In hindsight, I believe No. 4 was trying to save me from my own, er, persistence. And he may have been trying to protect his own mental health, or maybe his own marriage, for all I know, by taking that weekend off. I couldn't have been the easiest client and I think No. 4 was at the end of his rope too, with me, my case, and who knows what else. After all that I felt *guilty* by saying no to this laboriously achieved deal. And yes, that was another echo you just heard from my relationship with Dick, another thing I didn't realize until too late. Nevertheless, it was time to make a change.

My last instruction to No. 4 was to tell Dick that because the lien on my house wasn't removed, in addition to some other technicalities, this deal was nothing more than an agreement to agree. Because Dick and his shark thought they had a deal, they had let go of the trial date, which bought me the time I needed to find a new lawyer. This late in the game though, it wasn't going to be easy. Moreover, the shark was saying that this wasn't just an agreement to agree, and that I was in breach of an agreement between Dick and I, and was going to get a judge to award costs against me.

Really, I'm the one in breach? Huh, maybe she was right, but at the time all I could do was savour the irony.

[#]

After getting turned down by Lawyer No. 10 again, Lawyer No. 11 also turned me down, but not before telling me something really interesting. Many of the judges who preside over family law trials are not experts in family law – they may have more experience in civil or criminal cases. So the lawyer has to guide them through how family law is supposed to work, and the lawyer that can tell the most convincing story, the one who seems to be the superior guide, can influence the decision the judge will make. Another shocker for me – that the judge that may be assigned to my case may have to interpret the statute and the evidence with little experience. Which is another reason why precedent is so important in law, and another reason I was unlucky. With this new FLA, pickings were slim when it came to precedent, which made it more likely the judge would use the law down to the letter. This is also another reason to make sure I had the right kind of lawyer for the kind of fight I was in.

After delivering that bummer, No. 11 directed me to lawyers No. 12 and 13, who worked together and who both had their own shark-like reputations. They agreed to take my case, despite the lateness of the hour and all the odds stacked against me. Their intent was to pressure the other side to back off my pension if I turned over the funds from the house quickly.

That didn't work. "I get half her pension," Dick said, "that was the deal." Dick refused to budge - he wasn't getting as much out of the house as he wanted and was looking for another way to improve his retirement portfolio.

But for once, finally, time, and luck, would be on my side.

Shark No. 12 got an adjournment so he and No. 13 could get up to speed on my case. A new trial date was set but as Dick kept refusing to budge on the pension-split, interest rates started going up. When interest rates go up, pension valuations go down – I know, it confuses me too but I'll do the math for us later – and the longer Dick refused to settle, the higher interest rates got, and reducing his cut of my pension. The beauty of this was, it didn't matter what the judge said – the value was the value and according to law[61], Dick couldn't get more than half, whatever that half was.

While No. 12 and 13 were having a hard time finding a way to get me out of the previous deal, I knew that Dick wanted to move to sunny climes and live in a shack near the beach. It seemed to me that he was desperately afraid of getting old (who isn't, but it's worse for Peter Pans) and not being able to play the player on that beach. He wanted to settle quickly, get out there and on with his life, and needed immediately accessible cash.

This time, No. 13 and I, we boiled *Dick's* frog. Right before trial, No. 13 offers him an unlocked-in retirement savings rollover from my accounts, taxable to him and at a not insignificant discount, in exchange for him releasing his claim on my pension. It's midnight. Trial is tomorrow. And still, Dick comes back, again and again, demanding a few thousand more...

[#]

I realize now that a big part of my problem is that I kept expecting this system of law to be fair. Which turned out to be just another fairytale. Depending on who you ask, legislators' efforts to keep up with the times with respect to the ever-changing family dynamic has done more harm than good. In an effort to protect stay-at-home parents, now a deadbeat can roll into your house and your life and lay claim to half your stuff and, if they don't feel like working, claim spousal support to boot. Okay, maybe I'm oversimplifying for dramatic effect, but it can happen, because it did, to me. That's not the worst of it. More recently, federal lawmakers have been trying to shift away from awarding sole or majority custody to the mother in an effort to avoid parental alienation, mostly of the father.[62] While that may be laudable for the majority of cases, it has a dark side.

Courts struggle to establish fairness in high-conflict family cases, and much of it hinges on the credibility of the respective parties, where there can be a lot of back and forth, different versions of the same story, rife with conflicting evidence. But in an effort to be fair and impartial, to execute blind justice, great harm can be done. Researching this book, I read about a woman who worked hard as a teacher, bought and paid for the house she shared with her husband, who, unbeknownst to her, had a drug and gambling problem. When they split, he not only went after half her house and her pension but took her to court, demanding that she pay off his debts from his two addictions. And *won!* What if he beat her on top of it all? Wouldn't matter. She can press charges, but he'll still get half of all her stuff and she still has to pay for his debts. How blind is that?

And what if there are children in an abusive relationship? Let me be clear: I'm not anti-men,[63] but how is a woman mostly likely to die? At the hands of a current, or former, intimate partner,[64] usually a male partner. Okay, so you survive the abuse and get out of the relationship, but now the court tells you to share custody with the man who, unless you've managed to convince the police to convict (and good luck with that), bashed your face in. Your fears for the safety of your children could very well fall on deaf ears. In family law, justice is both blind and deaf.[65]

From other perspectives, changes to family law, irrespective of its disabilities, can be applauded. Because these laws mean that no one needs to stay in a cruel, toxic, or even unpleasant relationship just because they can't afford to leave. Or that a good parent can't be pushed to the sidelines, consigned to watching their kids grow up from a distance, just because of their gender. But these changes have also had unintended consequences, some infinitely more tragic than anything I experienced. I can't bring myself to write much about it, it's too awful, but please honour Keira and her mother by reading about Bill C-233 or googling "Keira's Law." If you or your children are victims of domestic violence or abuse, all I can say is that I'm so sorry for what you have endured, or are enduring, at the hands of a blind and deaf family law system. In these situations, a good cohab would not have protected you or your loved ones. I'm not sure what could.

[#]

"Family law is fucked up," Lawyer No. 13 says to me, her voice cracking. We are both so tired. It's been hours of Dick continually saying he won't negotiate before coming back "one more time." And us going back saying no, or offering a slighter bigger, but locked-in RRSP instead (there's plus and minuses). It's obvious how badly Dick wants to avoid the trial, and although I've significantly reduced the amount of money I have to give Dick, it's still too much to pay someone who broke so many promises.

But then No. 13 says, "Don't let it fuck you up any more than it already has."

And I say, "Okay. Done. I'm finally done. This time I really mean it. Let Dick have his pound of flesh. Because I have better things to do."

And I finally let it go.

But you can avoid what happened to me, before they move in, *and* after they move out. And who knows, maybe that solid cohab agreement can actually help keep you guys together. But before we get to that...

Here's Another Recap

What I learned about the Law:

It has evolved to protect the lower-earning spouse, regardless of the circumstances.

It's always changing, but not always keeping up with the times.

It doesn't protect you from empty promises.

It can't protect our boundaries unless we know what they are.

It likes to split things down the middle, no questions asked, unless you have an agreement that says otherwise.

It is precise and explicit, and allows judges to uphold valid contracts.

Your lawyer has to prep you for what's in store for you, especially once everything has unravelled.

It favours deadbeats.

If your lawyer isn't on the same page as you, you're going into a fight with one hand tied behind your back.

Everyone, including the lawyers, will do everything and anything to stay out of a family law court room

Know when to fight back, and when to walk away.

What I learned about Love:

That's it's really hard to find.

But not worth being so desperate for it that we are our own undoing.

The sooner we stand up for our boundaries, the safer we'll be, whether or not the relationship survives.

No one can be as cruel as someone who once said they love you.

The breakup will be as tumultuous, and as costly, as the relationship.

What you can do:

Learn the basics of family law in your jurisdiction before moving in with anyone.

Check in with a family lawyer before letting anyone move in with you.

Learn your values and boundaries before letting anyone move in with you.

When negotiating something that's important, don't let anyone call you petty.

Listen to your gut, not your Dick (or Dickette).

Love yourself first and best before trying to love another.

Have a relationship with someone who respects your values and your boundaries.

In your agreement, consider the outcomes from a breakup and terms that you can live with.

Don't let anyone become financially dependent on you

Don't agree to split things you don't want to split.

Don't let anyone—especially someone who says they love you —manipulate you into a trap where you flock yourself.

Don't fall in love with a deadbeat

Write an unflockably explicit, boundary-respecting cohab agreement!

PART THREE: KNIT A DIFFERENT FUTURE

CHAPTER 13: TWO LAMBS DON'T ALWAYS MAKE A EWE

As sociologist Stephanie Coontz writes in *Marriage, a History – How Love Conquered Marriage,*[66] marriage has always been a mercantile affair, until love messed everything up. A union based on mutual need and support (and, yawn, financial responsibility) is stable, whereas a love-based one is not. If I hadn't been seeking the "one" who could "complete me" I may have recognized the real motives behind Dick's passionate wooing. Moreover, if I'd read Dr. Coontz's book *before* I partnered, rather in the aftermath, I wouldn't have been so shattered by the realization that what Dick was really passionate about was someone who could improve his retirement portfolio.

The point is, no matter how badly we want someone in our life, how badly we want that march down the aisle, that family of four, that destiny of holding hands together forever until the sun sets on our lives, no matter how crazy in love we are, knowing the law, and more importantly *ourselves*, well enough to draft a decent cohabitation agreement, can not only save our financial future, it might even save the relationship. But that also depends on the partner you have chosen. And not all of us choose well. Which makes knowing the law, and ourselves, so important.

Whether we're entering into this union for love, financial security, or both, rather than an instrument of division, as many see it, a good, boundary-respecting cohab can help smooth the bumps that are surely a-coming around the bend in every relationship between creatures as complex and wonderful and flawed as humans can be. While we can't foretell the future, we can still think of your cohab as a tool to help protect our union, rather than as a knife to break it up. Especially if there are allowances for the changes that will inevitably come down the road.

But whether this works or not, I believe, also depends on how much you truly trust and respect each other. T&R is the glue that will keep every relationship going, especially during the rough patches that inevitably hit once the pheromone-driven mania has worn off (T&R doesn't matter that much during this phase because we're too busy having fun and great sex to get pissed off or worried about anything else). It's the foundation, the mortar between the bricks. Once we lose it, we've already lost our relationship, the way we lose someone whose brain has died but we can't bring ourself to turn off the machines.

If I could go back in time and advise my former self, if I could get her attention off of the dude she was so gaga about, it would be to ask her: *What causes you to respect someone? What makes you trust them? Why are you so gaga over _this_ person?* Are they triggering some deeply buried hole in your psyche (and if that's the case, are you headed for a trauma bond or codependency)? Or do you truly respect them? Do you truly trust them? And if you do, why? What is it about them that earns this incredibly valuable, hugely important, can't do without it, glue that will hold your future together... together?

Ask these questions as you draft your agreement. Hell, ask what makes you respect yourself, because that's the most important thing. Write these things down, along with your value-based boundaries, and sit back and take a good look at them. Do any of them conflict with your arrangement with your partner? Do any of them conflict with who your partner is or what you think they might do?

And this trust thing: how do you know you can trust someone? When some people distrust because of differences in religious beliefs, skin colour, vaccination status, or how you vote, how are you supposed to know whether you can trust your partner?

Well, you just do, or do not, as Yoda would say, there is no try. When you simply trust someone, or when you're not sure you can, that's your gut talking. Yes, T&R can bloom slowly, and sometimes you want to wait until it does. But like love, T&R can also erode over time, like the flow of water carving a stone. I trusted Dick when we drafted our cohab, I believed the promises he made, and then one day I woke up and realized I no longer did. Same with the respect I had. I once hugely respected Dick's adventurous spirit, his minimalism and resourcefulness, his knowledge of mountains and sea, his passion for the environment and the little guy. But after a few years, I felt like the cranky, bitchy caretaker of a middle-aged teenager rather than the bedazzled damsel in a whirlwind romance with the man of her dreams. And I suddenly realized, after Dick moved in and started lounging around my house in between part-time gigs and reading self-help guides on how to find yourself through yoga and tantric sex, that I was being taken advantage of. T&R, poof, gone! Go figure. I've heard it said that the reasons you fell madly in love with someone will be the same reasons you fall out of love with them. And lose that precious T&R.

So, if I could sprinkle some pixie-dust, go back in time, and talk to the Wendy version of myself about to sign a cohab with Dick, I would say, "Wendy, you want to take a chance on this Peter Pan? Fine, but ask yourself how much you are willing to pay when he decides it's time to pack up his toys and go home to Neverland. And put that in your cohab." Actually, what I'd really say is *"Do not move in with someone you don't truly trust and respect!"*

I know my Wendy wouldn't have listened—she was too much in love and having too much fun. I just wish I could have convinced her to future-proof my cohab a whole lot more.

> *"... love without esteem is capricious and volatile..."*—Jonathan Swift

Based on my experience, I going to cover what should be in a cohab according to what ended up being the most contentious:

1. Division of property, such as real estate and savings, and debt
2. Pension division
3. Spousal Support
4. Other stuff like wills, inheritance, pets, and living

expenses

Just make sure the agreement is fair to both parties and is reasonable. Otherwise, it won't stand up in court. You may protest that "reasonable" is in the eyes of the beholder. Certainly, what was fair to me (what you get is based on what you put in) was not fair according to Dick, and conversely what was fair to Dick (you pay, I stay) wasn't fair to me. But "reasonable" is also a legal term – a standard created to help courts and juries make decisions as to what is fair. An often-cited case of an agreement overturned due to being unreasonable and unfair is *Miglin v. Miglin*, where in 2003 the Supreme Court of Canada overturned an agreement that Ms. Miglin made with Mr. Miglin, waiving spousal support despite taking on full custody of their four young kids on her own with no prospects of gaining proper employment until they were grown. The court overturned that agreement and granted her spousal support indefinitely, even after the kids had grown up and left home, because given her parental responsibility she had no prospect of ever making as much money as her ex, who waived custody, could.

The court's decision seems fair in this situation, but what about mine? Or what about if Mr. Miglin wanted to share custody, or had wanted Ms. Miglin to keep working during their relationship, and Ms. Miglin said no? Now what? Family law and the legal system can only take you so far. You, your partner, and the agreements you make with each other, have to do the rest.

Here's what I learned about the Law: anything goes in an agreement, as long as a court finds it "reasonable"

Here's what I learned about Love: forget about the gaga - if you don't trust and respect them, don't let them move in

Here's what I learned about cohab agreements: writing one can help you figure out if you both trust and respect one another.

CHAPTER 14: MIND YOUR FENCES

I wanted to title this chapter "Why do we give away the farm then get really pissed about it later," but that was too long. So. Property division. It's probably one of the more contentious issues of family law and – in my experience anyway - closely linked to personal boundaries. Legal terms used to indicate what one party may owe the other include "compensation payment" or "equalization payment" for, "entitlement to", and "interest in" said property, which can include pensions (see the next Chapter).

Property is stuff you and your partner have: real estate, vehicles, bank accounts, investments, pensions, offshore accounts, RRSPs, that racehorse you won in a bet in Orlando...

Objection your Honour – I take offence to laws that consider non-human animals property.

Overruled – the law once considered slaves and a man's wife property so it obviously still has a long way to go before animals get a fair shake. More to the point, the law evolves very slowly, way slower than social norms, and family law – it seems to me – is still stuck on the *Leave it to Beaver* model of the family unit. Which doesn't include blended families or gray divorce, where people are coming together with stuff that has nothing to do with the other person. Which is why we can't always rely on it for justice, which is why proper agreements, and property agreements, are so important.

Regardless of what the property is, it breaks down into two basic categories:

Excluded property—stuff you had going into the relationship.

Family property—stuff that you got during the relationship.

On relationship breakdown in many jurisdictions, you keep the value of the property you had going into the relationship and split the rest. But wait... you might think that excluded property was excluded, as in not part of the deal at all, right? Wrong! The *increase in value* of that excluded property that occurred during the relationship *is* family property, at least in most provinces in Canada. Maybe that was not such a big deal at one point in time, but with the way real estate and other types of investments can skyrocket, this can turn into a really big deal, really fast.

It's the same with debt: the debt that we bring into the relationship and the debt that is accrued during the relationship. The first one is on us, and the second is split 50-50. Maybe not such a big deal in the days of supercheap debt, but higher interest rates can mean debt division can get ugly too.

Here's the kicker: those are the only two criteria. Stuff we had before we met Mr. or Ms. Perfect, and stuff we bought while we were with them. Doesn't matter, at all, whether they paid a dime or lifted a finger toward any of it; half of its value is theirs the minute they walk out the door, less what it was worth just before they moved in. Not sure you need some examples, but here are some anyway, with numbers similar to my experience, just to make the point and really freaking scare you.

Mary buys a house on her own valued at $800,000, with $300,000 down and a $500,000 mortgage. Joe moves in with her a year later. He helps around the house a bit but pays virtually nothing toward the mortgage or expenses. Five years later, they split up and the house is now worth $1.4 million (say this is in Vancouver or Toronto) and the mortgage has been paid down, by Mary, to $250,000. Without a cohab agreement that dictates otherwise, this is how the property division works:

The net lift in value is:

$1,400,000 – $250,000 – $300,000 (i.e. $800,000 – $500,000) = $850,000.

This net lift is to be split equally between the parties, irrespective of who paid the mortgage and expenses for that property. Ya, you read that right. Despite the fact that Dick, er, sorry, Joe contributed virtually nothing toward the expenses and upkeep of the property, he rolls out the door with $425,000. Family law says that's what he gets. It doesn't even matter that he slept with the maid, or smacked Mary around a bit.

But wait, it gets worse. Say Joe moved in with Mary *before* she bought the property, but everything else stays the same. Now the house is fully family property and here's the split:

$1,400,000 − $250,000 = $1,150,000. Divided by two, that's $575,000.

Now Joe rolls out the door with $575,000, despite contributing nothing, bonking the maid, and maybe he even kicked the dog. He gets over a half-million dollars for doing sweet F all toward the costs of the property, and it doesn't matter how awful he was to Mary, her paraplegic mother, or her dog. The judge ain't gonna give a damn.

And it gets worse! Say Mary tries to fight Joe in court, arguing that it's not fair, I paid for it all, he cheated on me, my mother is dying, the dog needs dental work, yada, yada, yada. And it goes on for two years until an agreement is reached. Now the house is worth $1.8 million.

Joe moved out two years ago, moved in with the maid, and contributed nothing to the house, which now has a mortgage of only $100,000 due to Mary's efforts. Okay, you might think that it's fair that the property be split based on the value at separation. Makes sense, right? He moved out, didn't contribute, Mary kept the place going, right? Nope, family law in some jurisdictions, like BC, says that property division is *at time of settlement in court*, regardless of the vagaries of market forces. So now the split is:

$1,800,000 – $100,000 = $1,700,000.

Divided by two, that's $850,000 dollars that Joe walks way with, and goes to live with the maid in a penthouse in Florida while Mary has to make do with a one-bedroom rental in a bad neighbourhood because she couldn't afford to pay Joe out on top of her mother's care and her dog's dental bills. Is it fair? Who cares? Too bad, so sad, says family law.

The amendment to my agreement with Dick attempted to make the division of my house based on financial contribution, using a rate of return model. Dick would reap the benefit of what he invested in hard costs toward my house rather than the huge number family law would give him. Using the first Mary-Joe example, if Joe contributed 50% of the costs over the time the net lift was $850,000, then he gets that $425,000. But if he only contributed 20%, then he gets $170,000, or 0.2 X $850,000.

For my situation, that could have been fair, but there are other scenarios family law takes into account. What if there are kids involved? Say Mary was an international lawyer who often had to travel for long periods of time but also had a pre-teen child from her previous marriage. One of the things she likes about Joe is that as a local carpenter, he rarely needs to travel and wants to take care of Mary's kid. He likes being a stay-at-home dad, taking his new role seriously enough to pass on some lucrative carpenter gigs because Mary is away and he needs to be around for her child. Mary's career soars, her child thrives, and Joe's career stalls a bit. Suddenly the property division exacted by family law seems more fair (let's say Joe was nice to Mom and didn't kick the dog). And that's because this is exactly what family law was designed to do: to protect Joes like this, not enrich the Dicks of the world.

And it still doesn't matter that Joe slept with the maid.

Well, actually, it could. I read about a case in the Court of Appeals of Indiana, where the couple had signed a contract agreeing that if the woman cheated on her partner, or failed to contribute to the maintenance of the property they lived in, she'd lose all interest in that property. As sad as it is that someone would need to put fidelity into a cohab (where was the trust and respect there?) the connection between the ex-partner receiving anything was *explicitly* tied to her fidelity and her contributions. Those were her former partner's boundaries, he drafted an agreement that upheld them and she signed it. After being impregnated by another man and terminating the relationship, she sought a share of her former partner's property and the court upheld the agreement.[67] Nothing needed to be interpreted; the judge's path was clear.

That's what your cohab needs to do – make it crystal clear what your boundaries are, and what you actually want.

But what about your partner's boundaries? The way they think they can and want to contribute? Or the way you need them to because, as in the previous example, you have to travel a lot and need someone around to take care of the kids, or Mom, or the house, or the goat in the backyard. Or, what if Joe, a carpenter, did a lot of work on the house. So much that he was responsible, in part, for its increase in value? Maybe his boundary is "my work needs to be recognized" and that recognition needs to be in the form of a slice of the value of that property. What are his remedies if Mary disagrees? Regardless of their cohab, he can still claim "unjust enrichment"—that Mary has been enriched by the fact that her house went up in value due to his efforts, and it's unjust because he didn't get a big enough piece of that action. If Joe had enough evidence (e.g., receipts, date-stamped photos of his work-in-progress or completed, etc.), he could establish what is called a "constructive trust," which is an equitable remedy (based on fairness) in which the court "constructs a trust" in favour of the non-owner spouse.

Dick gave the constructive trust thing a go – but for things like washing carpets, walking the dog, and raking leaves, so it didn't stick. It has to be big ticket stuff in order to sway the court. Nevertheless, a very good lawyer (VGL) is needed to navigate all this, one that can help you translate your and your partner's boundaries into a cohabitation agreement, but they rely on you to tell them what you can live with. That includes in the future, after Mary has slept with her Zumba instructor or Peter has quit his job so that you have to support him. I think when negotiating these things, we need to leave those rose-tinted glasses at the door. Look down the road, see where this will go given what you know and see about your partner today. Listen to your gut and honour your boundaries so this all doesn't end in tears or a terrible wine-and-chips habit.

A good cohab won't save you from making a bad relationship choice, but knowing your boundaries and striking a deal that honours them can save a promising relationship from going sour with resentments and bottled-up anxiety. In some cases, where people come together later in life, with their assets already established, a "no property split" deal may be the best. Reserve any division for those assets and debts obtained during the relationship, and base that on respective contribution. The parties can then divide the cost of living according to their means. That's what I wish I had done. If your prospective partner grumbles too much about that, then maybe he or she has an agenda you need to know about sooner rather than later.

And watch out for that debt. Debt accrued during the relationship, without a cohab, is split 50-50, whether you had anything to do with it or not. What if your partner, the one with the drug habit or the gambling problem, can't pay? It's all on you, babe. Happened to someone I heard about... lady who plays piano at her local church, fell in love with a dude from a faraway land—cute, sweet, jobless (why is that so sexy, Wendy?)—let him move into her house, had a couple kids, and he starts gambling. By the time she kicked him out, he was hundreds of thousands of dollars in debt with no means to pay. In the separation, the court ordered her to compensate his debtors, except that she couldn't because he took off for home with all of her money! Now the bank owns her house and she can't afford to retire. Like ever. Not to mention those adorable kids he gave her and refused to help support.

[#]

So, this is how your cohab could look with respect to property division. Which I suggest you write in plain-speak, which I'm using now, and pay your VGL to convert it into that cool, unintelligible legalese they use to ensure that your agreement will hold up in court (one hopes) should you need to take things that far.

Using the same scenario as above:

X. Upon separation, the property (Mary's house) will be divided according to the following formula:

(Net Lift Equity × Hard Cost Contributions) ÷ Total Contributions, where:

a)   Net Lift Equity = (Property Value at Separation – Mortgage at Separation) – (Property Value at Start of Relationship – Mortgage at Start of the Relationship).

b)   Hard Cost Contributions by Joe are according to Schedule A, and those by Mary are according to Schedule B.

c)   Total Contributions = Schedule A + Schedule B.

Y. But if Mary and Joe have children and Joe is the one who stays home to take care of them, then the formula changes such that:

a)   The Net Lift from the date of birth of their first child to the date of separation is divided equally.

b)   Unless Joe sleeps with his yoga instructor, in which case he gets nothing.

This is just an example based on the Indiana case, meant to illustrate that you can write whatever conditions you both agree on. That last item may not stand up in every court, but if that's your boundary then there's nothing stopping you from putting a condition of fidelity in your cohab, and it's up to your lawyer to translate that into something the judge won't throw out on spec. But then again, if that's how you feel now, as you sit down to write an agreement with this smiling, shiny person sitting across the table from you, you may want to consider writing a separation agreement instead. Because without trust and respect, you don't actually have a relationship, right?

Here's what I learned about cohab agreements: you can agree to divide your property, and your debt, any way you like, just check with a lawyer to make sure it can stand up to a court challenge.

CHAPTER 15: GREEN(YER) PASTURES

Ah, retirement: the golden mile, the sugar-white beaches, the emerald pasture, the broken shackle, the moment you've been waiting for, the tickets to Florida on the counter, the sun in your eyes, the sand between your toes, the breeze in your face during the perfect day at shuffleboard...

Barf.

Never retire, says Neil Pasricha, author of *The Happiness Equation*, and I believe him to be 100% correct, as do many in the Blue Zones,[68] places and cultures where people live longer and more meaningful lives, well past typical retirement age, whatever that is supposed to be. A concept that originated in Germany in the 1800s as a way to reduce Marxist power and to get old farts out of the workforce so young farts could have their jobs,[69] retirement, according to some studies, is a consignment to devolution, into irrelevance and a slow (and sometimes not so slow) death. Unless you have another job to do, paid or unpaid, a passion to pursue, a novel to write, pictures to paint. In which case, are you truly retired? Hell no, we won't go!

However one defines it, having financial security in our

"retirement" years is a good thing. If you're younger than thirty, this may not resonate with you yet, but pay attention anyway because one day it will. Because everyone should save for it as much as possible, especially as our life-spans grow. The thirty-somethings of today are going to the one hundred-somethings of tomorrow, and no one wants to be poor and old: either condition sucks enough on its own. If you are helping the planet in some way and not hurting it, I say there's nothing wrong with working toward a life where you get to pursue a career in alternative art form, volunteer at the local animal shelter, travel the world, become a best-selling author, excel at lawn-bowling, etc., whatever your passion-purpose turns out to be. Just make sure your efforts to do that are protected.

[#]

When Dick was wooing me, he knew exactly how to talk. For instance, he knew that he should say: "I'm going to get a job, with a pension! And help you pay for this house." Instead of: "I'm going to pretend to get a job, with a pension, for a while, and after a few months I'll quit to basically hang about the house walking the dog and planning the vacations you'll pay for while you work your butt off to keep things afloat. And you watch your step because if I get tired of you, I'll take half your shit when I leave."

If he'd said the second thing to me, I wouldn't be writing this book because I would've shown him the door then and there. At least I sure hope so (I was still a Wendy at that point, so who knows). For a few years I allowed myself to accept his excuses, his reasoning - for why he wouldn't be paying his fair share after all but still deserved his chunk of my assets - but it ate at me and fed the fire that turned me into the Seven-Year Bitch. I even said to him, the night we broke up, "I feel like the mother of a seventeen-year-old" in a middle-aged body. It wasn't until years later and after many therapy sessions that I figured out why. Peter Pans are often pretty good at pretending to be Dudley Do-Rights, but only for as long as it takes for Wendy to give them the keys to the castle.

Many of my friends and family thought Dick was using me. They tried to warn me, subtly, too subtly as it turned out, because I defended Dick so vigorously, desperately trying to hold on to the last shreds of the trust and respect (T&R) for him that I had built on a stack of lies. But over time, over the months and years of watching my unemployed partner excel at dog-walking and painting the front steps, spending more time at keeping track of how much my house was worth than trying to find a proper job, while I worked full-time, contributing to a pension, saving for the future, paying the mortgage, paying the taxes, paying for the car, the repairs, the insurance, the vet bills... those last shreds of T&R slipped through my fingers, slowly, too slowly, for me to save myself from what was coming.

But none of that matters in the court of family law, which says I had to fork over half my pension anyway, and perhaps a healthy dollop of spousal support while I was at it. Nor did it care that Dick had two pensions when we signed that cohab: the other was from his previous work to which I was not entitled because he had quit before he met me. I think it's ridiculous that someone with two pensions can grab a chunk of yours, but that's family law for you. So, if you are lucky enough to have a job with a pension, treasure both because like love, these things can be hard to find.

Pension Division

How pensions are valued and divided can be complex and difficult and I urge you to consult with an expert on what kind of pension or savings plan you are contributing to and how it will be divided if you separate from your partner. Then take that information into consideration when drafting your cohab. That said, here's what I learned, and wished I'd known before I signed mine.

Whether you think that's fair or not, pensions are generally considered divisible family property in the event of a breakup, on both sides of the border[70]. Not every job is pensionable. Teachers, federal employees, provincial employees, and some private company employees have pensions, but more and more privately employed people have stock options or other types of retirement savings plans. Or it's up to the individual to maximize investments such as Registered Retirement Savings Plans (RRSPs) in Canada, or, in the US, 401(k) plans, which are similar to Canadian Group Retirement Plans, or Individual Retirement Accounts (IRAs) which are the US equivalent of an RRSP. All were set up by governments to help people save for retirement and many are administered by an employer. If it's not a "pension," then it's considered "property," and division is treated in the same way as a house. But an employer-administered pension is a particular kind of asset, and is typically divided in half for the value over the period of time the two partners are together.

Which makes sense when you have kids and one partner stays at home to take care of them while the other goes to work and gets a salary and accrues a pension. Up to 50% of the employed partner's pension, accrued over the course of the relationship, goes to the other partner. No questions asked. Whether children are in the picture or not. Unless you have an agreement that stipulates otherwise.

At the risk of sounding cynical—okay, that ship has sailed, hasn't it? —I recommend that you keep records and proof of cohabitation, *regardless of whether you're the pension-holder or the spouse of one*. I learned of a case where a woman lived in a spousal relationship with a man with a government pension which would have been fairly generous. They were together for a long time and she took care of him when he was ill, despite a few periods of separation. Because she didn't keep records of the times when she lived with this man, and didn't keep proof such as her mail sent to his address, she couldn't prove the relationship to the government's satisfaction. When her partner died, she got nothing and later died in relative poverty. As unfair, if not more so, as Dick being able to take my pension when he had his own.

A good cohab could have solved both injustices. In my case, for instance, pension division should've been contingent upon him maintaining the job he'd had when we got together. I didn't know you could write something like in an agreement! Worse, my lawyer didn't tell me I could. But I'm telling *you*. If that's what you want, and your partner agrees, there's nothing wrong with putting something like that in your agreement, especially for a later in life union in which you're not raising kids.

But what if Dick was truly a loving partner, like the

woman I told you about, who cared for me when I was ill? Maybe he forwent pensionable employment so he could stay home and take care of me. What then? Is it still fair that he gets nothing? I would say no.

Under reasonable circumstances, pension division can make sense. If you're making good money, it's worth considering that pension income is taxable. If you have good income from other sources, punting some of your employment pension to your ex-partner makes that their taxable income, not yours. Also, depending on how old you are when you separate, that pension is future money that you may never see. I mean, God forbid, but let's face it, there are a lot of ways to die between now and retirement so you might want to consider dividing that pension rather than coughing up cash, which would *not* be tax-deductible, by the way, at least not in Canada. Another something your lawyer should help you understand.

Types of Pensions

It's also very important to understand what kind of pension you actually have. You are likely to have the more typical *defined contribution pension*, which means that the amount you pay into it is defined. A more rare type is a *defined benefit pension*, which means that the amount you receive at retirement is defined.[71] Great if you can get it, the defined benefit pension is declining in popularity due to the cost to the employer. In Canada, we also have the Canadian Pension Plan (CPP), which is divided between spouses in family law unless an agreement stipulates otherwise, and Old Age Security (OAS), which is not divisible (but may come into play when spousal support is worked out).

Different types of pensions are divided differently, depending on the administrator of the plan. For example, some provincial plans make the ex-spouse a limited member of the plan, where they receive a portion of the benefits paid to the contributing spouse.[72] In some cases, the plan does not provide benefits to an ex-spouse until the contributing spouse has quit, retired, or passed away. Meanwhile, Canadian, federally administered plans divide immediately and provide the ex-spouse a lump sum right away, to be deposited into a life annuity account, which is an account the ex-spouse can draw down a set amount each year for their life expectancy. I can't stress how important these differences can be when negotiating a settlement. I didn't understand that my pension administrator provided the immediate lump sum and that I had no choice in the matter, and neither did the lawyers advising me. If I had, I may have made different choices during my settlement negotiations.

Spousal Rollovers

Depending on your partner, your boundaries, and your taxable income, your employment pension may be an asset you want to leverage when it comes to settlement rather than a straight-up compensation payment. So an option is to buy your ex out of their "interest" in your pension with a spousal RRSP rollover. This is a tax-free instrument allowing you to provide your ex with a lump sum, based on a valuation of their chunk of the pension, in exchange for letting you keep your pension intact for when you retire. Or it can be a combination of both. And you can put these eventualities into a cohab agreement so you both know what will happen to that pension when—sorry,

I'm so jaded now—*if* you separate.

Unlike RRSPs and real property assets, pensions can be sneaky. It's money that disappears from your paycheque, month after month, year after year, secretly growing into an asset that can make a huge difference to your lifestyle when you retire. They are easy to ignore when you make a deal with your partner, easy to blow off as something you don't need to worry about as much as the value of your house or your exposure to spousal support. But depending on what kind of pension it is, and what the rules are on how it's divided, you could end up on the hook for a big chunk of change. If it needs to be divided as a lump sum, the pension administrators calculate an annual annuity and then use a discount rate and the number of years your ex is expected to live to determine the present value required to give them that annuity annually for the rest of their expected lives.

The formula is:

$$PV_{\text{Ordinary Annuity}} = C \times \left[\frac{1 - (1 + i)^{-n}}{i} \right]$$

where:

PV = present value of the annual (ordinary) annuity
C = cash flow annually
i = discount rate (based on interest rate)
n = number of periods (in this case, the years your ex is expected to live).

For example, if the pension administrators determine that Dick is supposed to get $10,000 per year from my pension, and the discount rate is 4%, and he's expected to live another 25 years, that lump sum is $172,920. That's the amount you have to pay back your pension providers, and they will take it out of your pension cheques, month after month, even if your ex dies way before you do. In other words, you'll be paying your Dick/Dickette for the rest of *your* life, not theirs.

Some ex-spouses will want the cash up front and may be willing to settle for a smaller lump sum, and if you can afford to pay them out, you can keep your pension. But depending on how old you are, that may not make sense. What if you're sixty with a family history of heart disease or cancer? Hate to say it but you may never even see a dime of your pension, in which case it may make sense to let your ex take it.

The point is, don't ignore it. Like failing to listen to your gut, ignoring your pension's quietly growing value can lead to a horrible surprise down the road.

I ignored it. My employer pension was growing with every paycheque but I was so terrified about the growing value of my house and the fact that I'd lose it if Dick ever walked out the door. I was too worried about getting stuck paying spousal support I couldn't afford because he refused to work. I was so focused on preventing my savings from being sliced down the middle for a grasshopper who refused to save for the winter. I forgot about my pension and that I had agreed to divide it. It was so small when Dick and I first started to cohabitate that I didn't protect it, even as it grew. A mistake, among others, that I regret to this day.

Here's what I learned about cohab agreements: don't forget about your plans (and savings) for the future, and only agree to divide them if it makes sense for your relationship.

CHAPTER 16: IS DICK MILKING EWE?

Apparently, some states in the US (according to the Internet, which is never wrong) still allow adultery to be a reason for not paying spousal support. But in most jurisdictions, a no-fault separation system is in place, meaning no matter how nasty and awful and deceitful your ex-partner was to you, even if they cheated on you and slapped you around, and kicked your dog, they can still get half your shit and spousal support to boot. And that can happen even if there are no kids involved. Are you horrified? So was I, when one of the letters from Dick's lawyer demanded spousal support.

According to Canada's spousal support guidelines,[73] for couples without kids, support duration ranges from one-half year to one year of support for each year of cohabitation. So, for Dick and me that would have been almost seven years. But for some couples, spousal support can last a lifetime.

Insanity! some of you may say. But remember, family law was designed to protect the partner who sacrifices career and earning potential to not work in order to take care of family, not protect your assets from an opportunist. What if Dick and I had had children, and he'd sacrificed a lucrative career, a big salary, and years of contributions toward his retirement in order to give them a stay-at-home parental experience? This is called *compensatory support*. The second type of support in BC is called *non-compensatory*, which is determined based on the needs of the lower income spouse. Other jurisdictions have similar mechanisms.

Spousal support isn't mandatory but it is common when there is income disparity, and to compensate a spouse for care of children. Formulas for determining amounts and duration, for couples with and without children, are provided in Canada's federal guidelines[74] and can vary according to state laws in the US. But why, you may ask, does family law even allow this kind of division when there are no children? What if one partner just decides that they don't need to work or contribute? Well, it just does, so it's up to you to write your cohab appropriately. If you don't, there are avenues to take after the fact,[75] but why ask for that cockfight?

Whenever I asked Dick to find full-time work, he would always say to me: "At this point in my life, I just wanna do what I wanna do, and let you pay for it." Well, he didn't have the audacity to say that last bit out loud, but that was the reality. But let's turn it around and imagine for a moment that Dick really meant well, tried his best, but just didn't have the earning power that I did. Despite his best efforts, he couldn't match what I spent on our lives together, felt bullied by my wanting him to contribute more than he felt he could and belittled by reminders that he wasn't pulling his weight toward the household, and eventually left because he felt disrespected and unappreciated. No one should be made to feel unequal or treated poorly just because they make less money, or because they are a stay-at-home parent. Yet many couples struggle with this. Inevitably one of us will make more money than the other, and financial disparity is a major contributor to tension and relationship breakdown—among the top five reasons, according to some researchers,[76] after infidelity and lack of commitment. No wonder, given the power imbalance it can create.

What this means is, should a family member stay home to take care of the kids or the household, then spousal dependency is an inevitability that both parties should recognize and talk about early on, making sure they are on the same page with respect to its ramifications and whether this is within both of parties' boundaries, no matter who chooses to stay at home. Ironically, Dick and I did that, and I was very honest about my expectation that we both get jobs and keep them, that I didn't want to be in a relationship where one partner is financially dependent on the other, and he agreed. But then I let myself be manipulated into signing the first (and faulty) cohab agreement that basically gave away the farm.

Meanwhile, the family law system is encouraging the non-earning spouse to become financially independent as soon as possible, or so Lawyer No. 4 told me, and a chapter is devoted to this topic in the federal guidelines for spousal support in Canada. Also, as you can read in Leena Yousefi's article, spousal support is not automatic. Your ex may need to demonstrate financial need or entitlement to compensation as a result of being in a relationship with you, or as a result of that relationship ending. And, as always, an agreement between the two of you can trump all, by stipulating what you pay or whether you pay. For example, in *Thompson v Young*, 2014 BCS 799, Young sought to have an agreement for no spousal support overturned, but the court was "not persuaded that the respondent suffered any significant economic disadvantage arising from her relationship with the claimant or from the breakdown of that relationship. Nor [was it] satisfied that she has suffered any significant economic hardship arising from the breakdown of her relationship with the claimant."[77] Young was denied spousal support, despite Thompson making significantly more money than she did.

But here's another kicker you need to know: Kids or no kids, if your ex turns sixty-five within five years of your split, you're on the hook for spousal support. For. The. Rest. Of. Your. Entire. Life. And that's on top of the pension thing. Yikes!

Researching this book, I learned of a couple who after twenty-five years of marriage, split up when the kids left home. She hadn't worked much and since she's turning sixty-five within that five-year window, he has to pay spousal support for the rest of her life, or his, whether he retires or not. It could be argued that this woman has no hope of being self-supporting after being a stay-at-home mom for most of her life, but in other cases the reasoning isn't so clear. Like another case I heard about, where the guy is still paying his wife support for a marriage that ended twenty years ago, even though she now has a good job and is married to someone else who makes as much money as her ex. Where's the logic there? If there is any, it certainly escapes me.

Except that it almost happened to me. Dick, who turned sixty the year I showed him the door, gave it the ole college try, turning out his pockets, quivering his lip, and asking the court for spousal despite of the no-spousal support clause we had in our cohab!

Objection Your Honour – How did two people who seemed at one point to be so much in love get at each other's throats like this? More to the point, how could this lady become so full of contempt for this man she once claimed to love so much?

Sustained - I know, it shocks me too sometimes. But then I realized something, with the help of the VBP I worked with. I already touched on how relationships are dynamic and fluid, but so are the people in them, subject to each other's forces and movements. We change each other—back and forth—the entire time we are together. My VBP likened it to a Mobius strip or a pair of electric snakes grabbing each other's tails, where the pulses of your energy and being send current through your partner and vice versa. I believe it is even possible for Wendys to become Petras and Peters to become Wendells, depending on the relationship they are in. I was more of a Petra with my ex-husband, for instance; because he took charge of everything, I atrophied. But I began my transmogrification into a Wendy almost the moment I met Dick.

Freaky stuff! And in the face of such drastic change and evolution, how can we future-proof a cohab agreement?

I would say, based on my experience, you probably can't. Not completely, anyway. There are lots of things that can change between people during the course of a relationship: jobs, children, homes, health, etc. Some of this stuff we can control; some we can't. What I wish I had done is built in some protective clauses, triggered by a big event such as—gee, I don't know—

Dick quitting his job? The point is, realize that the arrangement you make today may not reflect the circumstances, or your partner, of tomorrow.

Here's what I learned about cohabitation agreements:

1. I would ask my prospective partner that they keep a job - don't become financially dependent on me

2. If we separate and my ex partners with someone else, either through common law or legal marriage, any spousal support from me ends

3. If I have a pension and they don't, I would ask my partner to start putting some savings into an RRSP. (That way, you are both saving for retirement and there are two assets to split in the event of a breakup)

4. If the partner refuses to, or can't, save for retirement, then I would ask they waive their rights to my pension, or to agree to an unequal split, (*especially* important if you don't agree with their position), assuming no children are involved (if we have kids, and my partner is the stay-at-home parent, then I would agree to the 50/50 pension split)

5. If I have a higher-paying job and my partner wants to pursue their dream of being a singer-sensation on YouTube or a world-famous screenwriter (guilty!), then will they sign a waiver on spousal support, with the provision to make changes as the family changes or grows (for example you have kids, dependent parents, or adopt some very large animals)?

Here's what I learned about Love:

If your prospective partner says no to these types of requests, Yoda has some questions for you. Just don't do what I did, which was justify, make excuses, and play the One Day Wager.

What you can do: I think it all comes down to this. Don't be afraid to be you, and you alone. Love yourself first and most. Being on your own is not that bad. Especially when you compare it to some of the alternatives.

CHAPTER 17: OTHER CHOPS OF LAMB

Your VGL should make sure you're covering all areas of family law in your cohab, but how these are covered depends on you. In my case, my cohab did a good job on these items, except for the first one. Which can, admittedly, be pretty sticky if you're moving in with someone with less income than you.

Living Expenses

My original cohab was pretty light on this topic because Dick wanted to avoid this conversation like a Carolina Reaper and I was still in gaslight mode. All my cohab said was "the parties intend to be self-sufficient and contribute substantially equal amounts to the costs of their joint household". In my experience, this was not specific enough because Dick never paid anywhere near 50% of our living expenses.

I'd be okay with paying more if my partner is doing the best they can, but if they're taking advantage of me, that's a different story. I've seen some cohabitation agreement templates that go as far as having a spreadsheet of expenses and the parties expected contributions. While this may be more typical of non-spousal cohabitation, it's something to consider. And if you decide you're okay with paying more on a regular basis, which I ended up having to do, put in a caveat to prevent such unequal contributions to living expenses from establishing a pattern of dependency, which can leave you open to an obligation to pay spousal support.

I would say that unless you're living with a dick, an open, honest conversation about who pays for what and how much, and having it all down on paper, can diffuse a lot of conflict over what can be a divisive issue. Just be honest, with yourself especially, and as specific as possible about what both your capabilities and expectations are.

Wills

Nobody likes these things, but *it was very strongly impressed upon me to* write a will at the same time as the cohab. No matter how young and healthy you are. This is part of future-proofing your assets and your relationship, making sure everyone feels safe and fairly treated, including other family members. A cohab outlines how you will govern your relationship, and what happens if it ends. Your will governs what happens to all your stuff if you're no longer around. Everyone should have a will, and *especially* if you have dependents, whether they have legs, wings, or paws. And having stuff like this written down is especially important for blended families, where certain people may not be protected by the law. If you don't have a will and you leave them high and dry, then, sorry, you're the dick.

Drafting a will is also a good time to ask yourself important questions, ones that bubble up from your boundaries and your concerns for those you love. Do you want your partner, or your kids, or your sibling's kids, to inherit your house? If you want to keep the house in the immediate family but at the same time you don't want to see your partner turned out of their home, a workaround could be to let your partner live in the house until they die, then will it to be sold and combined with the rest of your estate. It's also a good opportunity to ask your partner some important questions about their expectations, which could be important if you have kids from a previous union.

The important thing to note is that without a will, things may happen to your stuff that you wouldn't have wanted. Such as the government keeping your money rather than it going to your partner. Or a Dick/Dickette getting your house rather than your kids.

Survivor Benefits

In Canada, your ex-spouse may be entitled to benefits, depending on the plan being divided, for example Canada's Pension Plan, as well as other factors. If you're that plan member you may have other intentions for those benefits once you are gone. There are many permutations to be considered but ask your lawyer about including this in your cohab as well as your will.

Inheritances

An inheritance from a third party is excluded[78] in most of the jurisdictions that I checked[79] (make sure you know your jurisdictional *FLA*, I can't say this enough times), but it can depend on how you treat it. Keep it separate. Put it in an investment account and do not mix it with other funds. Never, ever put gifted or inherited money toward the family home. As soon as you do, it becomes family property and is divisible. If you inherit a house, or your parents give you one, don't move into it with your partner. Even if you have a cohab stating that that piece of property is excluded, your partner could argue in court that it's now family property and divisible if you both lived in it. So if that's a concern, rent it out instead, and live elsewhere with your partner, preferably where you both pay your fair share of expenses.

According to family law firms in Ontario and BC,[80] you shouldn't even use inherited or gifted money to pay down your mortgage, as a down payment, on a home line of credit, or on renovations for the place you both live. If you do, you will no longer be able to exclude that money if you split.

Gifts and Windfalls

BC's *FLA* treats gifts and windfalls similarly to inheritances and considers them excluded unless they are transferred into a form of property that is divisible, such as the examples given above. But there are also the gifts that you make to your partner, or they make to you. What about those?

BC's *FLA* is structured such that what happens between two parties, financial or otherwise, during the relationship is mostly irrelevant. All that matters is what you had going in and what you acquired during the relationship.[81] Which means that the thousands you spent on vacations, the time you paid for a new car, and all of that appropriate footwear you bought for your partner doesn't matter. Just like it doesn't matter how many times they walked the dog or took out the garbage. You can divide these things as you see fit in your cohab, but I'd focus on the big-ticket items. Asking for someone to pay for their shoes won't win you any sympathy votes with your lawyer, and probably won't look too good to a judge either.

Pets

When Dick and I split up, I had a horse and a dog. The horse was worth a bit of money and Dick was really attached to my dog. But here's where his reluctance to shoulder responsibility saved me. I think he really loved the dog but couldn't (or wouldn't want to) take care of her, so he didn't fight me for custody. And he'd never spent a dime on the horse or took care of him, which was well documented, so again no fight there. But other couples have fought bitterly over who gets the fur-babies—just read the tabloids—and in some cases the poor animal can get pulled like taffy in different directions.[82] What really saddens me is that the law in most jurisdictions treats animals like property (just like women were treated not so long ago, remember?), and not like family members, so relying on a judge could mean the animal does not get the best home.

I don't even like the word "pet" but that's a topic for another book. While some jurisdictions, like Rhode Island[83] and the province of BC[84] are in the process of changing family law so that "pets" no longer fall under the category of "chattel" in order to allow judges to consider the animal's welfare, as of this writing those changes have not yet been put into the law. Don't do this to your fur-babies, as the breakup will be hard enough on them. If they are your pets when Dick/Dickette moves in, keep it that way by putting that in your cohab. Don't wait for it to all unravel because that's a shit-show and a painful whirlwind you don't want to endure, let alone put Fido through it.

Here's what I learned about cohab agreements: make sure you consider *all* aspects of cohabitation and separation, in life and in death

Here's what I learned about Love: never forget about Fido, who will always love you first and best.

CHAPTER 18: DON'T GET UNRAVELLED

As NASA can attest, even the best laid plans can go awry and so here you are, where all systems have failed and you are hurtling toward annihilation. You tried your best, you loved them the best you could, you wrote the best cohab you could, but it didn't take, or the soulmate turned into a jerk, or maybe simply decided they didn't want to be with you anymore.

The first thing to do is to decide what is most important for you - the kids, the house, the car, the boat, the Air Miles, the cottage on the island, the German showjumper, the family dog, or a dream to bike around the world - and how those priorities will be supported, financially. What do you need to hold on to, in order to make the rest of your dreams, now that this "happily ever after" has ended, come true?

Whatever your situation, whether you're negotiating a cohabitation agreement or a separation settlement....

1. Take your time.
2. Heal from past (or current) trauma
3. Negotiate like it's a business deal (yea, I know, but that's what everyone will tell you)
4. Know your values and stand up for your boundaries

5. Pick the right lawyer and make sure you agree with their strategy.

I did none of those things, got horribly unravelled, and the only people who profited were the lawyers. And in the end, Dick.

Take Your Time And Heal

If you are like me, you may feel lost, heartbroken, traumatized, and as if life has no purpose or meaning. You may experience anxiety, depression, or worse. If that's where you are, try to wait as long as you can, or at least until you feel stronger. Because you'll be negotiating a separation that you don't want, at least not yet, and from a perspective that will not serve you.

I think anyone going through a split can benefit from counseling, especially if you have trauma, extra-especially first-family trauma, the trauma that led you to a dick in the first place. I sought help from several mental health professionals - including the one who told me to go on a dating app, which is how I got into this mess - before finding one who helped me find the learning in this painful experience, the good that will eventually come of it, even though it was impossible to see at the time. When I started seeing the VBP, I was so wrapped up in grief and anger that all I saw was a bleak and black future. But she helped me turn this into a journey of personal growth, healing, and learning, showing me how to reshape my vision for the future into one of hope and adventure. But it took a long time. And a lot of work!

The price for freedom was a tortuous path, but a relatively short one compared to standing on broken glass for seven years.

So, if you've been abused, traumatized, or even simply Wendy'd, talk to a therapist before you talk to a lawyer, or at least at the same time if your situation is urgent. Ask your lawyer to find you some time to heal before you have to walk onto the battlefield.

If your ex is driving you toward court because they want money or whatever, and you aren't ready, ask your lawyer for as much time as they can give you to heal. On the flip side, remember that you have two years from separation if common law, and from divorce if married, to file a family law claim.[85] As we saw in my case, court dates loom but they are often delayed for all kinds of reasons. Adjournments are very, very common, and even opposition lawyers are likely to grant them if a halfway decent reason can be provided. No lawyer wants to look like an relentless jerk in front of the judge, especially when they are likely to face the same judge when it's their turn to ask for a delay.

I felt a lot of pressure from the court dates and applications Dick threw at me in his quest for coin but I should have taken a deeper breath. A VGL can find a defendable reason to adjourn if you need more time. Most judges are measured and fair, and reticent to force a final order on someone who just isn't ready. That was my experience, anyway. Two judges rejected Dick's lawyer's applications to get money as soon as he wanted it, opting instead to make sure a fair deal had been reached between two people ready, or as ready as they could be, to reach it. So unless it serves you or your dependents, don't feel pressure from your ex and their timeline to settle.

And maybe, in the end, you'll decide you don't need to do

battle. Perhaps you will find the place where you *can* reach a settlement with your ex; that perhaps they are not such a Dick/Dickette after all and will meet you halfway so you both can get on with the rest of your lives. Maybe even be friends one day, say hi at the kid's wedding, babysit each other's grandkids, with wives past and present drinking 'tinis at the beach and giggling about how you mismatch your socks…

Or not. For some of us, this rosy, bird-chirpy scenario is unlikely. My ex, whether he was a narcissist or not, had to prove he was the righteous victim he believed himself to be. And if he was a true narcissist, he wouldn't be capable of any empathy. It's like being born without a limb or sight – it's just not there. So how do you settle with someone like that? Whatever your decision, fight or settle, try to make it wisely, from a strategic rather than emotional place. In other words, don't do what I did.

To Mediate Or Not To Mediate

The Internet is full of self-help for the heartbroken who have been tossed aside by someone, and it's a balm to the soul to be told "Don't worry about it, honey, he (or, more rarely, she) was a narcissist and you are much better off without them." In a few cases that is true, but only a small percentage of the population is actually diagnosed with this personality disorder, while a lot of us can have narcissistic tendencies to varying degrees. Narcissism, according to my research and experience, comes with a heavy side order of anxiety and depression and needs constant attention and excitement in order to fill an empty soul. This can take many forms, usually involving risk—drugs, sex, mishaps, and misadventures—anything to fill them up, get some attention, and make them feel special. A complete inability to perceive and understand the beliefs and positions of others is another symptom—only their view, one in which they are the centre of the universe, or the victim of everyone else's cruelty, matters. How this can manifest in a relationship is the love-bombing they do in the beginning, where they tell you over and over that you're the most amazing, beautiful thing they have ever seen and they have been searching for you for their entire lives. They need to believe this as much as you do, and how dare you disappoint them by turning out to be a mere human.

I believe humans are narcissistic as a species. If we weren't, we wouldn't have a handful of billionaires while billions of children are starving, we wouldn't have 5,000-square-foot homes while people live in the streets, we wouldn't have people driving SUVs in the face of climate change, we wouldn't vote for despots who gain popularity by promising to persecute other people, we wouldn't have so much pollution and loss of natural habitat and the other species that need it, or Facebook. Sorry, I'll get off my soapbox now, but the point is, we are all capable of narcissism, to the degree that we hurt those we once loved. It's a protection mechanism: I want to leave her so she must be a loser and bad in bed. I fell in love with my exec assistant because my husband is so pathetic and clingy and I need a real man in my life. And this labelling turns into a lack of empathy. We are doing this to them because they deserve it, not because we are selfish assholes.

Which means any of us can act without mercy, without empathy during a breakup. If anger and resentment has built up to that point, can collaboration and mediation actually work?

I don't know what it takes to be a skilled mediator, I only know I spent $6,000 on one who hadn't spent enough time on figuring out what buttons to push, where the hidden hurts were, why there was so much anger and "shag you" going on. Part of the art of getting from no to yes is figuring that out, for both parties, and a small hurt soothed by a gesture can go a long way. For instance, if Dick had acknowledged how much I had put into the relationship and the house and the finances, if he had apologized for not keeping the promises he had made in the beginning, if he'd offered to meet me halfway between the old cohab and the new one, I would have been less revolted over giving him a chunk of my assets—still nauseated, mind you, just not as much. What I'm saying is, it could've moved the needle. It could have ended right then and there. What I'm saying is that you have to know who, and what, you're dealing with before you agree to mediation because otherwise you are just wasting time and money and a lot of emotional energy for no gain. At all. Well, except for the lawyers and mediator. They get paid either way.

The Lawyer That's Right For You

Which is another oddity of law, if you ask me. If you hire a contractor to build you a house, and they fail to complete, do they get paid? No. If you buy a car and the engine doesn't turn over, can you tell the salesman to take it back? Of course. But when a lawyer says, "Hey, let's do a mediation." And you say, "What's the point, the guy's a dick." Then the lawyer says, "Oh, the judges don't like it if you don't at least try mediation before trial, so you better do it." And it turns out to be a total waste but you have to pay for it anyway. Another unravelling reality I wish I'd know about before going into the boxing ring.

So don't do what I did, which was to automatically go back to the lawyer I'd previously worked with. For the cohab I went back to No. 1 who'd helped me so much during my divorce, whereas I should have found a lawyer more like No. 10. For my split with Dick, I went back to No. 4 who'd tried to help with the amending agreement, whereas I should have hired a lawyer like No. 13. Think of it like buying a car: do you want to save gas, take several kids to school then soccer practice, or drive up a mountain in the snow? Depending on your needs, you pick the type of vehicle that will get you there. If you want to drive up the side of an icy mountain but try to do it in a compact hybrid, you might end up, well, dead, possibly—but you'll certainly be out of pocket for a result you didn't want.

"Test-drives" (aka "consults" and not free) where you explain your case and get the lawyer's feedback on likely outcomes and their strategy for achieving the result are a really good idea. Also, you can get recommendations from people who've driven this "car" before. Or read the lawyer's blogs or publications, if they have any, to get a sense of where their priorities are as a practitioner. Your therapist may even be able to give you some names - if they counsel people going through separation and divorce, they may know some lawyers with experience in your situation. Another option, which I did when I changed lawyers, is to pay a senior lawyer for a consult on my case and which lawyers might be the most suitable. Lawyer No. 11 told me how trial lawyers guide the judge toward the desired outcome through persuasive argument, how the better the persuader can win the day, before recommending the last lawyer (yay No. 13!) that I hired to finally get me through this.

Communication is key. If your lawyer doesn't communicate with you, doesn't give you options, doesn't give you time, doesn't give you all the information you need to make a decision, not just when the rubber is streaking the road but *always*, then maybe this isn't the right lawyer for you. Don't forget, you're the customer who is paying a lot of money for their time. Get your money's worth or get out. I'm not saying Lawyer No. 4 wasn't good at the legal stuff—he was - and I also believe he boiled my frog in an effort to save me from myself. In fact, sometimes I wonder why he didn't fire me! But at times he treated meetings with me like they were unnecessary, that I was a pain in the butt because I was fighting the inevitable. Every lawyer can have an off day, but if your lawyer makes you feel like a pain in the butt more than once, start shopping. You are paying way too much money for anyone to make you feel that way.

Finding the right lawyer can be daunting so ask for recommendations from friends, colleagues, and your therapist (that's how I found some of mine).

Ask senior lawyers for recommendations for more junior lawyers with some experience with your type of case.

Create a short list of at least three lawyers to speak with (or more if your case is complex or highly contentious).

Write a list of issues that are important to you (e.g., communication style, how involved you want to be) and discuss these with each prospective lawyer. If a lawyer doesn't tick your important boxes, move on.

Strategize a plan that you and your lawyer can be on board with.

Ask your lawyer about preparation for any court process, including discovery. Don't let them wing it or spring anything on you

Ask your lawyer what their strategy is when getting close to trial. 90% cases settle outside of court[86], usually close to trial so don't be blindsided in a forced settlement like I was. Talk to your lawyer about this: are they going to let things get to the stroke of midnight? At this point, you're in a game of poker. Know what their strategy is for when things get that close to the wire

If you actually are going to court, ask your lawyer to prepare you as early as reasonable, not a few days before trial

Remember that this is a business relationship. The lawyer is not your friend and not your therapist. Be as calm and collected as you can whenever you deal with them, and cry on someone else's shoulder.

Back To Boiling That Frog

Here's the other thing that really unravelled me. Often the "last ditch effort" at a deal is just to get you hoping for it, enough that you stay at the negotiation table when your ex comes back with: "I'll see your offer and raise you ..." and, if your ex really is a Dick, that raise will be something a lot more than what "you can live with." Now, things can get ugly. Especially when no one wants court but you. Both lawyers may try to scare you with all kinds of horrors, such as:

> "Your house is worth so much more now than when you split, you could lose it." [87]
>
> "Sure, judges don't like to overturn agreements, but you're questioning the cohab too"
>
> "Let's see how much you'll owe him if the judge decides to divide using the *FLA*"

I believe No. 4 was genuinely concerned about the judge splitting the house value as of at trial, rather than at separation – a critical distinction in a volatile housing market, like Toronto or Vancouver. BC's FLA, on valuation of family property and debt reads:

"Unless an agreement or order provides otherwise and except in relation to a division of family property under Part 6,

(a) the value of family property must be based on its fair market value, and

(b) the value of family property and family debt must be determined as of the date

(i) an agreement dividing the family property and family debt is made, or

(ii) of the hearing before the court respecting the division of property and family debt"

So, No. 4 was right. If I lost my case, I'd lose my house, and a lot more besides. But he couldn't convince me that the judge wouldn't care about how Dick had treated me during the relationship, and the dickish things he'd done, such as with his pension. No. 4 may have been trying to save me from furthering my own destruction by forcing me to settle, but even shark-like litigators don't want to enter that courtroom if they can avoid it. It's better to maintain control, said Lawyer No. 12, which is code for doing a deal on the courtroom steps rather than step inside the lair of the almighty and the capricious. Better to split it down the middle rather than face the uncertainty of a judge who may be having a bad day, who may be more concerned with the murder trial they have to deal with tomorrow, or may be the judge your lawyer has to face again, in a different trial, down the road. Judges like lawyers who avoid their courtroom, is the impression I got, and lawyers need the judges to like them so they can win their next case.

So now you're faced with a counteroffer that is more than what "you can live with," probably a lot more, but maybe less than your worst day in court. Now it's your turn. But your lawyer won't let you counter with anything that's less than you already offered, so now you've crossed a line in the sand that you swore you never would. And then your ex counters again... and so it goes, inch by inch, until every line you ever drew in the sand has been crossed and double-crossed. And yet the pressure doesn't let up. They've made their final offer. "It's this or *trial!*" the shark thunders. "How *dare* you, Wendy, turn down my client's most unnecessarily generous offer to settle in order to save the judge's precious time and taxpayers their hard-earned wages, while you continue to be an intransigent, stubborn, selfish cow!" but in melodically indignant legalese.

Now all eyes are on you. Are you going to be the Dick now, Wendy? Are you going to be the one scuttling a halfway reasonable deal, Wendell? When it's just a few thousands dollars more? How petty are you? Then the bell will start to ring, with everyone banging on it. *Bang, bang, bang... settle, settle, settle*: that's what they all want you to do. Your collaborative lawyer. Your ex's shark lawyer. Even your new shark lawyer. Maybe even family and friends, who have grown tired of hearing what a dick your ex is and how unfair family law is. Most importantly of all, the judge you'll face if you don't.

But remember that almost *all* family law litigations settle before trial.[88] The assistant to one of the lawyers I hired, won't say which one, told me that in her experience, in all the years she'd worked for that firm, only one of their cases ended up in court. That's something else I wished I'd known before I started my fight – that I wasn't on a highway to Judge Judy's courtroom. Instead, I was actually jockeying for - or rather being maneuvering into - the pole position for a pistols-at-dawn settlement deal.

I can't emphasize that enough. If I had been better prepared for that reality, I wouldn't have been so freaked out by all the negotiations just before trial. More importantly, I would have spent way more effort and money prepping for negotiation, rather than for trial. Hopefully you never find yourself in my position but if you do, now you know what to expect. And that's the real reason I ended my 5-year relationship (5 years, really?) with No. 4, because he didn't prepare me for these realities. Or maybe he tried to but I was too focused on getting my day in court to listen. Either way, we'd lost faith in each other and just like with Dick, it's better late than never to unravel a relationship in the hopes you can darn a better future.

Is all of this to say, my dear Wendy or Wendell, that you

must cave to the system? Pay because you played? No. Well, maybe... but also that so much of this could have been avoided if only you knew about it before you wrote your cohab. In my case, we're talking about a sheep that's already left the barn. It's too late for me. But you, you still have a chance. And if you know about how it could all unravel, then maybe you can knit yourself a different future. Because family law doesn't protect you. You think it will, but it won't. Because if you're the one with the job and the assets, it wasn't even made for you.

Here's what I learned about the Law: it's not about the fight for what's right or for what's fair, it's about how to settle outside of a courtroom

Here's what I learned about Love: any one of us can become a narcissistic ass in a breakup

Here's what I learned about cohab agreements: protect yourself from lovers who turn into asses by future-proofing the heck out of it.

CHAPTER 19:
RAM V. EWE

Not all of us have the luxury of too much time, when your well-being is at stake or children are involved. Sometimes there are other factors, like rising real estate prices or fluctuating investment markets, where settling quickly can make the difference between keeping your house or losing the farm, or the opposite. In these tumultuous economic times, who knows what the perfect timing is? If they claim to, well, let's just say there are lots of con artists out there. But say you've taken enough time for healing and self-care to avoid unravelling yourself, you've hired the right lawyer, you are as steady as you can be, and ready to make the right decisions.

The previous chapter was about making sure you are on the same page as your lawyer about strategy to achieve your goals, and this chapter is about the tactics used to get there. Some may be used against you, or some can work for you, and may be stuff not every lawyer will tell you about, and certainly more things I wish I'd known about before I wrote my first cohab with Dick. Whatever you decide to do, in case you're in a fight you did not want, here are more things about the law I learned in my struggle to hold on to what I had earned.

Unjust Enrichment

Lawyer No. 10 (my favourite one) told me about *unjust enrichment*, which means that someone receives a benefit that corresponds to a loss to another that has no basis in law. To successfully claim unjust enrichment against another person, a claimant must prove three things:

1) The person received a benefit
2) The claimant suffered a loss corresponding in some way to the benefit
3) There was no juristic reason for the benefit and the loss.

Juristic reason means there is a law-based explanation for the enrichment of one person at the detriment of another; for instance, a reasonable agreement or set of circumstances that allowed for the enrichment.[89] If this is absent, the courts may provide a remedy or reduce the benefits a claimant receives. In my case, it could be argued that Dick was unjustly enriched by being able to pay off his condo by living off of me. But because he didn't share with me the proceeds of the sale of that property, unjust enrichment could be used to reduce the amount of award he received from my property.

But unjust enrichment is tough to prove. For some examples of unsuccessful attempts, read *P.N.K. v. C.L.*, 2013 BCSC 1856, and *Harris v. Duin*, 2018 BCSC 1144. In my case, Dick's enrichment was not significant enough to make a dent in his claims against me, at least in Lawyer No. 4's view. I still wonder what a judge might have said.

Constructive Trust

Constructive trust is a type of unjust enrichment, such as the scenario where carpenter Joe made such improvements to Mary's house that it improved its value.

> "A constructive trust is imposed where unjust enrichment has occurred. Unjust enrichment is established where there has been an enrichment to the defendant, a corresponding deprivation to the plaintiff and the absence of any rationale for the enrichment. If those three requirements are met, a constructive trust is imposed."[90]

If Dick made significant improvements to my house, to the point that it increased in value, I would be the one who was unjustly enriched to Dick's detriment if he didn't receive an adequate share of the property. For an example of a successful constructive trust claim, see the Supreme Court of Canada case *Soulos v. Korkontzilas*, [1997] 2 SCR 217, which was not a family law case but indicates under what circumstances this kind of claim can be successful. Dick's claim, which included things such as cleaning carpets and stuffing takeout containers up my chimney to stop a draft, was not convincing to either his lawyer or mine.

Detrimental Reliance And Promissory Estoppel

Just like a contract, a promise is a promise, and beware of

those that you make. *Detrimental reliance* (thanks again, Lawyer No. 10) occurs when someone trusts someone else's promises or assurances and is injured because of that trust. Detrimental reliance is related to fraud: when someone lies to you, says they'll do this and that or give you this in exchange for that, then tells you to eff off after you've held up your end. But like unjust enrichment, it can be difficult to establish.

An example is *Sabey v. Rommel*, 2014 BCCA 360, one with a personal connection. A multimillion-dollar horse farm in Langley, BC, was owned and operated by Dietrich von Hopffgarten, a highly respected dressage trainer (whom I took lessons from), and his wife, Kim, a talented competitor. Sansouci Farm was a dream come true for both and a go-to place for equestrians across Canada, until Dietrich and his wife died, one after the other and unexpectedly. A few years prior to her death, Kim had reportedly promised the property to her working student Jesse Sabey, in exchange for less or no pay. However, prior to this alleged agreement, the couple had willed the property to their friend Burgi Rommel. When the dispute went to court, Sabey was initially awarded the farm on the basis that he had detrimentally relied on a dead woman's promise to will it to him. But Rommel successfully overturned Sabey's award in BC's Court of Appeal because Sabey was unable to convince the appellate judge of his detriment. In other words, the monetary damage Sabey endured as a result of the Von Hopffgartens' promise was insufficiently tangible for the appellate judge to uphold the award.

A successful example, also involving an equestrian property, is *Linde v. Linde*, 2019 BCSC 1586,[91] where a judge ruled that it was reasonable for the claimants to expect they would inherit the ranch they were promised, given the numerous assurances they received from the respondents, and their ability to provide proof of their labour and monetary investment. They were successful in a claim of unjust enrichment to boot.

Note that both these cases fall outside of family law. So far, I have not been able to find a successful claim for detrimental reliance in BC's family law courts, but perhaps someone who reads this will be able to point one out to me.

Promissory estoppel is "the doctrine that a promise made without the exchange of consideration is binding and enforceable if:

> The defendant made a clear and unambiguous promise
> The plaintiff acted in reliance on the defendant's promise
> The plaintiff's reliance was reasonable and foreseeable
> The plaintiff suffered an injury due to reliance on the defendant's promise."[92]

Well, hello, Dick! I was totally injured as a result of his endless promises of love and commitment. I would never have allowed him to move in had he not promised to maintain a job and a pension, to contribute to our home, to at some point sell his condo to pay down the mortgage, to get married in a few years, and on and on his promises went. None of these promises materialized, not a one, and yet I signed an agreement with him on the basis of them, and was injured—in more ways than one— as a result.

Here's the rub. I had to prove all of that. That can be tough, even if you're not dealing with someone who is being deceptive. Because we all say all kinds of things and make all sorts of promises when we're trying to get into bed with someone. But even so, there's something extra-special about someone who so deftly manages to cash in on lies and broken promises. So how do the courts remedy this?

Well, mostly, they don't.

Lawyers and the courts try really hard to stay out of our bedrooms and the promises made to get inside them. And unless the detriment is concrete and provable - like "I gave up a lucrative career making $200,000 a year to be a stay-at-home caregiver," versus "He wooed me then broke my heart and robbed me of my dreams of living happily ever after" - it isn't easy. Especially when you don't have an executed agreement, let me tell you. Despite all the evidence I had, it wasn't a slam dunk. Even though there's something in BC's family law called:

Section 92

It was Lawyer No. 10 (I loved her) who told me that, in BC's *Family Law Act*, section 92 upholds verbal agreements. *FLAs* in other jurisdictions have something similar because it's based on contract law, which says that verbal agreements are as binding as written agreements:

> *"The fact that an oral agreement is not in writing or not witnessed is not a bar to its validity under the FLA. There is no requirement under s. 92 that the agreement be in writing or that it be witnessed. Oral agreements*

*respecting division of property are enforceable if properly
proven on the evidence: Asselin v. Roy, 2013 BCSC 1681,
at para. 132."[93]*

But again, only if they can be proven. If both parties are
honest and willing to acknowledge the verbal agreement, no
problem. But if you're dealing with someone who doesn't do
that, it will depend on the evidence and on you as a witness (in
other words, don't be an emotional babbler like yours truly).

Dick denied the existence of our verbal and unsigned
agreements. Why wouldn't he? Words have no meaning in the
legal system unless they are backed up by tangible evidence. He
gambled that my testimony and documentation wouldn't hold
up in court, and it turned out to be a smart move because that
(and my aforementioned emotionalisms) spooked my lawyer
into forcing me to settle for more than those agreements said he
was entitled to.

Here is another scenario, just to flip it around a little.
What if your partner promises that if you give up your lucrative
career as a plastic surgeon to stay at home to take care of the kids
so they can go on to become a world-famous marine biologist,
they'll give you half of their multimillion-dollar inheritance in
the event of a breakup. But they don't write it down. We don't
need a written agreement, they say. You're the mother/father
of my children and I'll cherish you forever. And they're so darn
cute and sexy that you believe them. Years later, when they've
taken up with their scuba-diving instructor and have left you
high and dry, family law gives you some things, but not half of
that inheritance. You would never have given up your career if
it weren't for that promise. Especially now that you're over fifty,

have been out of the game for twenty years, and can never get back to the earning power you once had.

This is detrimental reliance and section 92 wrapped up in a shabby little bow. But only if you can prove it.

Agreements To Agree

Some agreements aren't technically agreements.

> *"Although uncertainty and incompleteness are distinct conceptual notions, their application in contract law is often intermingled. Incompleteness refers to parties failing to indicate adequately by their words or actions, objectively determined, that they have completed an agreement. Uncertainty, on the other hand, presupposes that the parties have in principle reached an agreement, but it is impossible for the court, within the rules of evidence, to give any clear or substantial meaning to their bargain. In practical terms, both uncertainty and incompleteness create problems regarding enforceability, since a court cannot make a contract for the parties where they have not sufficiently indicated what their intentions and expectations are.... Accordingly, the failure of contracting parties to agree on one or more essential terms will prevent the creation of a binding contract."[94]*

Dick and I had more than verbal agreements – the original cohab then the amendment, legally drafted and acted upon by both of us for several years. Yet Dick's lawyer managed to convince lawyer No. 4 that she could prove it was only *an agreement to agree* - such as in *Berthin v. Berthin*, 2016 BCCA 104[95], where the court found that the difficulties posed by trying to implement the agreement made it unenforceable.

But that's a knife that can cut both ways. As I mentioned, on the eve of trial I was backed into a corner where I had to settle. Because the offer letter that I got boxed into contained some vague terms and deficiencies, like the lien on my house, I argued that it could be interpreted as an agreement to agree, which may not be binding. One such case was *Bawitko Investments v. Kernels Popcorn*, 1991,[96] where the court found that, because all the terms of the deal were not determined, there was no meeting of minds and therefore no contract. In my case, that finalizing process turned up some stuff I didn't want to agree to so I wanted out of the deal, saying it was an agreement to agree and therefore not enforceable.

In my case, the settlement deal had sufficient detail that my attempt was not successful. But the irony was too delicious not to give it a try.

Change Lawyers

Your lawyer is a contractor, just like someone you hired to reno your bathroom. If they insist on installing a pink bathtub with flamingo taps and you want a post-mod glassed-in shower, you'd fire them, right? Just don't leave it until it's too late.

I'm not suggesting this as a tactic to delay proceedings. If the judge decides any of your moves are a tactic, things are unlikely to go well for you. However, sometimes the lawyer who was right for you when this journey started, is not the right lawyer for you on the courtroom steps. Before, you may have wanted a lawyer who was capable of enticing the other side to see yours. Now, if you want to save that house, you may need a street tough.

Changing lawyers can have an adjournment side effect. Most of the time a judge will assume you had a good reason to change lawyers and give you the benefit of the doubt. But not always. If they catch a whiff of a tactic, there's a risk that jumping from the chestnut stallion to the bay mare just before the wire won't hit the pause, slo-mo effect you are hoping for. Don't forget that the new lawyer will need time to get caught up on your case and what they're dealing with opposition-wise, and not every judge will grant this grace. But if you're wondering whether you should try another lawyer, then my advice, based on what happened to me, is that you probably should. At least get a second opinion (or a third, fourth, fifth...).

Read Some Case Law[97]

This is another piece of advice I desperately wish someone had given me before I let Dick move in with me, and certainly before I decided to fight his family law claims. You may say, *that's what I'm paying my lawyer to do*, but your lawyer, no matter how good they are, is not as invested in the outcome of your case as you are. Both lawyers, yours and your ex's, and the judges you will encounter, all rely on the judgements of previous cases - legal precedent. Because no one wants to have their butt hanging out there for making radical decisions, not in politics and not in law. If you can find cases similar to yours where the judgements went your way, stack your deck with them because your ass is already hanging out there and a resolved case could save it. Just make sure you stick close to your jurisdiction as much as possible. A judge in BC's Supreme Court[98] may be swayed by a decision made by the Supreme Court of another province[99] or the Supreme Court of Canada, but probably not from districts in other countries.

An example of a case you could bring forward, if you find yourself in a situation like mine, is *Dennis v. Gill*, 2018 BCSC 1533,[100] where Dennis sought unequal property division because she'd paid for almost everything, including two condos, while Gill contributed only marginally while living in one of them, even after they split up. Rather than a 50-50 division, the judge excluded some of Dennis's assets and divided the rest 75-25. Her ex still got too much in my view (by this point, none of us should be surprised), but the judge ordered an additional $10,000 be awarded to Dennis as a rebuke of her ex's misconduct. A paltry sum perhaps, but sweet nonetheless!

What was not so sweet: despite her ex contributing nothing toward her career or pension, he still got half of it. Another pearl of wisdom I wished I'd had before signing my cohab. Take a look at *Hamill v. Dunlop*, 2016 BCSC 1337,[101] if you need more convincing.

A more encouraging case to refer to is *P.N.K v C.L.*, 2013 BSC 1856, which I read with great interest as P.N.K. sounded like a Mr. Chancer after my own dear Dick, where the claimant's contributions to property and relationship were so trivial that the judge invoked section 95, which allows for unequal division of pensions, RRSP, and real property if equal division is deemed significantly unfair. Why didn't that work for me? Because of the cohab I signed when I wasn't listening to my gut. Sometimes a bad cohab can be worse than no cohab, but that's a *real* roll of the dice. What if C.L. had gotten a different judge?

Read The Fine Print

Whether you've hired a lawyer to protect you from what I went through before or after your relationship has ended, I can't stress enough the importance of doing your own due diligence. That means read, and understand, everything that is put in front of you. If you don't understand something, make your lawyer make you understand. Ignorance of the law and your liabilities are rarely a defence, especially if you have legal representation, and when, these days, so much information is available to us.

Now, I know that a lot of you will ignore this bit of advice. Either you're in the throes of crazy love and this cohab business is just a pain to be gotten over with so you can get back to having margaritas and sex on the beach, or you're in so much distress you want to crawl into a hole and let your lawyer wake you up when the nightmare is over. I know because I've been in both places. First, by ignoring the advice of No. 2, who tried to caution me about how I was agreeing to split my house (how I wish I could go back in time and apologize to her!) and then, much later, by rolling into a wine-soaked ball when No. 4 put a settlement offer in front of me on the stroke of midnight.

I'd learned my lesson by the time, with my new lawyer, we got close to a final settlement. I insisted on reading every single document related to transfer of assets and compensation payments, and again caught Dick trying to gain his chunk of my house without releasing the lien on it. Oversight or something not so innocent? All I know is if I hadn't caught it, I might have had another legal battle to fight.

Read every word. Carefully. No matter how distasteful. Whether it's a cohab or a separation agreement, whether it's a transfer of assets or a release of claim. *Every word.*

Get Creative

There is creativity within the law, such as leveraging constructive trust, detrimental reliance, unjust enrichment, but there's also another kind. I've used the word negotiations a lot here but the truth is, I didn't really know what that meant until very recently, when, as part of my job, I took a course in multilateral negotiation. I learned about different negotiating styles, and that it was possible to master all them, moving from one to the other as the situation required. One of my first thoughts was – OMG, what I wouldn't give to have had this knowledge when I was trying to get a cohab agreement I could live with, and certainly when Dick and I were wrangling for a separation deal.

Too late for me but I recommend getting at least some education on negotiation techniques before attempting to reach an agreement with someone you love, or once loved. Not to encourage you to find ways of manipulating the other party, but just so you recognize when it is happening to you, so you can decide what to do about it, and have the tools you need to react and take charge of the situation.

In the course I took, after recognizing the different negotiation styles, we learned to identify whether or not there is a zone of agreement by evaluating what is critical to us and to what extent, and what is crucial to the other party and to what extent. In my case, I didn't want to pay Dick money for the house he hadn't contributed a lot to, while Dick felt he was entitled to hundreds of thousands of dollars because my house had increased in value while he lived with me. I didn't want to pay out on my pension because Dick had reneged on his, while he felt he was owed that money because of our relationship. And neither of us, for the longest time, could budge from those positions.

If both parties value the same things equally highly, it can be difficult, if not impossible, to reach an agreement, and in those cases a judge may need to decide. But there are many ways to find a way from "No" to "Yes". Most lawyers and mediators are trained in these techniques and if you've got a good one, they will chart a path towards an agreement both parties can live with. But it's up to us to educate ourselves about what's really going on, to recognize what negotiation techniques are being applied, to realize that our lawyers have been trained in negotiation as well as they have been trained in the law, and whether we are being manipulated into something we may later regret.

Even if your Dick/Dickette turns out to be a creep/creepette, complete with scales and a nictating eyelid, they are still the person you once loved very much and knew so well. You know what makes them tick. What they really want. What this conflict is really about. If Dick had taken that advice to heart - apologized for his broken promises, acknowledged my contributions, offered to meet me halfway - I may have gone for it. My offering Dick, who wanted a quick exit and ready cash, an RRSP rollover is another example.

So. By utilizing a few of the tools and tactics the law allows, I was able to inch myself closer to a deal that would at least leave enough fleece on my skin to not freeze in winter, and, more importantly, keep my house. My beloved, ancient house. I'm sure many a condo developer was hoping I'd have to sell, but I managed to save it. And to those of you who may be saying – hey girl, it's just a house, my response is – I'd rather save my home than keep a dick.

Know Your Last Card

Like that awesome Kenny Rogers' song, at some point you gotta know when it's time to fight, turn and run, when to hold your cards, and when to fold like a stack of 'em. The important thing is to understand how the law works for you, and against you, so you can decide, with the advice of a VGL, how to fight back. And whether you have a hope in hell to fight back, because some of you won't, and some of you can't, depending on your cohab or lack of one.

What my last lawyer actually told me, the night before trial, before I finally let it go, was that no matter if, or how hard, I fall in love again, "Family law is fucked up so don't let it fuck you up more than it already has. And promise me that you won't move in with anyone else unless they have more money than you!" You can't blame her for seeming jaded.

On that note, let's go back to writing that cohab, because given family law and its legal process and all the other stuff I've been writing about, that's really *the only tool you have*. Because your gut isn't going to protect you—you'll be too much in love or in lust to see straight, let alone listen to what and who you should. Your family isn't going to protect you—your first-family issues are the reason you fell in love with a dick/dickette in the first place. And I hope by now you can see that your lawyer, no matter how good they are, can't protect you because they are handcuffed by a system that wasn't created for you, the Wendys and the Wendells of the world.

No, Wendy/Wendell, the only thing that can possibly protect you from this horror show, to save you from getting fleeced like I did, is writing not just any cohab, but a damn good one. But first, understand your values, your boundaries, your first family issues, any guilt trips you're on, the future you want for yourself, and put aside any soulmate true love rom-com bullshit you might be high on... and THEN write it.

Here's what I learned about the Law: for Wendys and Wendells, it's fucked up.

Here's what I learned about Love: same deal.

Here's what I learned about cohab agreements: a promise is a promise, but only if you can prove it.

CHAPTER 20: WRITE YOUR COHAB FOR EWE

In family law, there are all kinds of agreements—prenups, cohabs, amendments, contracts, settlements. When drafting any of these, don't be a victim of your past experience, your past relationships, your guilt, and your vulnerabilities, but be aware of them so that no one can take advantage of them during negotiations. According to sociologists like Ms. Coontz – successfully married herself for decades - that is what stable marital unions are: business and brass tacks, all subject to negotiation. No matter how many songs and rainbows and roses all those rom-coms spew at us.

> *A marriage makes of two fractional lives a whole;*
> *It gives two purposeless lives a work,*
> *And doubles the strength of each to perform it.*
> -Mark Twain

Your cohab is your roadmap, and you and your partner can travel that road any way you like. You could ask that one of you swing from a backyard trapeze yodelling Backstreet Boys every Thursday at 9 p.m. if they are to receive spousal support in the event of a separation. Whether a court finds that reasonable is another story, but there's nothing stopping you and your partner from agreeing to that. More realistically, you can stipulate that, upon separation, there will be no discussion of property division until you've had a chance to get some counselling, or go on vacation, or run with the bulls—whatever you need to get your wool straight. One of you can even write that they can sit about the house not lifting a finger for years or contributing a dime and still get half your house... oh wait, sorry, forgot for a sec. They don't have to write that into their cohab because, according to family law, that's the deal they already have.

The biggest thing that jumps out at me? The importance of stuff that the lawyers don't talk to you about: boundaries, foibles, first family trauma, false hopes, gaslighting, emotional predation, and so on. And why would they? That is not their job. It's yours, and your VBP's, if you need one, to figure that stuff out. I didn't, and suffered legalized theft as a result.

Start by googling "Family Law Act" followed by your

province or state. Most of them are online these days, and most of them contain the basic elements of property division, including pensions, debt, child custody, spousal support, and guidance on agreements, contracts, and fairness, or lack thereof, such as unjust enrichment. And then...

Listen To Your Gut

Love is huge. We all want it, so badly, too badly in most cases. So badly that we'll throw ourselves under the financial bus trying to hold on to it. Because it's nicer to listen to the pretty words being whispered in your ear, feel that caress along your inner thigh, and ignore what's really going on. But your gut sees past stuff that your loins cannot. Listen to what it's telling you. If your gut is niggling you that Prince/Princess Charming might turn into a Dick/Dickette down the road but you want to give this relationship a chance anyway, like I did, there are ways to make your gut (but maybe not your Dick), happy...

What that can look like:

Ask your partner to keep a separate address for a while so you both can do a "dry run." This would be a residence where your prospective partner, or both of you, spend a certain amount of time to avoid triggering the common-law condition. At least until you get to know each other better.

Draft an initial agreement that there is no division of property or debt and no spousal support, where both parties are 100% financially independent and agree to leave with the same assets (including growth of the same) that they came into the relationship with, even if you get married.

Add clauses about events that can trigger renegotiation of certain sections (e.g., if you decide to have children, get married, buy property together, or just because you feel like it).

Remember Family Law Favours Deadbeats

Maybe that's not a fair way to describe your partner, but I can't tell you how many times friends and family expressed shock and disgust that Dick was going after me for my pension and for spousal support. "That's outrageous," they would say. "He's a grown man with his own pension." "Why doesn't he get off his ass and get a job?" "You guys don't have any kids." "Let him try…" Etc., etc. These people—bless their supportive, decent-minded selves—had no clue what the law says and what it allows people to do.

Family law favouring deadbeats is the unfortunate fallout from the law trying to protect spouses that stay at home to take care of family. You could take Lawyer No. 13's advice and not get involved with someone who has no assets or can't maintain a good job, but yeah, that didn't sound very romantic to me either. All I can say is I threw that caution away for that romance and lost my wool sweater, or part of it anyway, and lost years of my life fighting back against what felt like a scam. A better, boundary-reflective, cohab would have saved me from all of that.

What that can look like:

List both of your assets and debts and their value at date of cohabitation, right down to the boat you are going to retire on and the credit cards you bought it with.

Exclude property from division (e.g., the house you bought, the condo your partner already had, the vehicles you owned when you met, etc.).

State whether you intend to split the increase in value (e.g., if your partner is helping pay your mortgage, and to what extent).

If you are going to divide property/assets, describe on what basis divisions will be made, for example, on the basis of financial contributions.

Define what constitutes a significant contribution, financial or otherwise. Does walking the dog and taking out the garbage count, or will it be something with measurable value like adding a third bathroom to the house?

Know Where Your Fences Are

In Hollywood those boundaries would be the first thing to bounce on the way to happily ever after. Because boundaries are boring and unromantic, right? But, in real life - which is where we are, I think, although who can tell anymore - knowing yourself well enough to protect the things that Hollywood finds so boring can save you from a lot of heartache and financial destruction.

Your list of values and boundaries may be different from your partner's. How different? Well, that can be a bellwether for how successful this relationship will be, for one thing. But the list can be about anything —your kids, how you spend your time, whether you need to go to church or donate to charity

—anything that matters to you. Not all of this will end up in a cohab agreement but it can shine a light through the legal murk and the clouds that will come when your partner pushes back with their own boundaries, needs, and desires. Knowing our values and boundaries allow us to move towards sustaining a healthy relationship long after the pheromone-madness has subsided. Even though we might have to bend a little on a boundary or two, for someone we love.

Remember Your Greener Pastures

However smitten and in love/lust you are right now, remember your future, and the future of your children if you have them. One day there may be a pension, and it may be very large, having grown silently in the background while you toil away trying to hold your job, your household, your relationship, and yourself together. And your ex will get half of it. Maybe they deserve it, maybe they don't, but family law doesn't distinguish between that spouse and the chancer looking for an easy ride. *They are both the same person in the eyes of the law.* So you owe it to your future self, your kids, and/or other members of your family to protect that asset too. Think about it not in the context of today, when you're young and healthy and all besotted with love, but tomorrow, when one of you decides to become a background vocalist for a Roma folk band. Or the tomorrow when you may really need it, because you are ill or unemployed or want to make someone else you love a beneficiary, and discover that it's just not there.

Decide If Spousal Support Makes Sense For You

One of my lawyers (the ever-creative No. 10) told me over and again: "What happened in the relationship doesn't matter one whit in family law court." That means it won't matter who walked the dog and took out the trash, or slept with who, who paid for all the family vacations and the cars and the mortgage. Unless you have an agreement that says otherwise, it's down the middle for everything the FLA considers to be family property, plus spousal support if warranted.

Unless you are okay with paying spousal support, don't move in with somebody who won't financially support themselves. Did I say this already? Well, I'm saying it again! We are so conditioned by the media to think that true love trumps all and who cares if Prince/Princess Charming earns a dime or not. Just make sure that's how you truly feel (boundary check!) *because if you support them financially during the relationship, you will have to continue to financially support them after it ends.*

I don't think enough people think about that. I certainly didn't.

If you have decided that one spouse stays home to take care of the kids, that's the reason for financial support as per family law design. But if that's not the deal you signed up for, for example if you are older and there are no kids to care of, then either state it in the cohab that there will be no spousal support or don't let them move in with you. According to the lawyers and my own experience, those are the only two choices. And even then, the judge can overturn the "no spousal support" clause depending on the circumstances. It seems to me, no matter how you slice it, you take a chance when you cohabitate with someone who becomes financially dependent on you.

Some things you can do:

Include a clause with an estoppel (a sanction) to prevent either party from claiming spousal support, no matter the circumstances.

Stipulate a time limit on any spousal support claim and/or limit the amount paid out.

Include a clause that both parties agree to maintain employment.

Keep your finances separate, including debt.

Stipulate that any money provided to the other is a gift, not meant to indicate nor create any dependency.

Don't Get Penned In By Petty

A boundary-reflective cohab - kind of sounds like a superhero's magically protective uber-strong cape, capable of deflecting the most avaricious of barbs, doesn't it? That's cuz it might well just be! But even with those superpowers, gaslighting can put you off your game and lead you to unravel yourself.

Remember that an agreement that includes an offer and acceptance, made without duress and through legal representation, is very likely to be upheld by the courts, even if it doesn't serve you. When negotiating your cohab, stand by your boundaries. If your partner can't respect them, and especially if they are resorting to manipulation, rather than understanding and compromise, to get you to agree to something you'd rather not, then you might want to ask yourself what they are really in this relationship for.

Ask yourself:

> What are my values and boundaries and how well do they match my partners'?
>
> Are these value-reflecting boundaries reflected in your cohab?
>
> Don't sign anything that crosses a major boundary (or your partner's) because it will be your undoing later.

But if you're like me, your wounded inner child might get in the way of stitching that protective cape properly, or maybe you just believed the lies you were told. And now your imperfect, non-boundary-reflective cohab (#hashtag fail on the superhero thing) didn't do what it was supposed to, there still are some things you can do even after the sheep has left the barn.

Be A Ram, Not A Lamb

Remember the basic premise of contract law is offer and acceptance, so don't let anyone force you into a deal if your gut tells you it stinks. Don't agree to a cohab (or a separation agreement) that doesn't reflect your beliefs of what's decent and fair. Family law costs us dearly *because of* our anger and *in spite of* our pain and grief—unless we protect ourselves with knowledge. Not just about the law, but about ourselves.

As Mr. Voss[102] would say, "Don't Split the Difference!" even though family law, in my experience, loves to go there

Don't accept something you don't 100% understand. Read every word. As Fox Mulder might say: Question Everything!

Don't assume your lawyer will save you—only you can do that

If you and your partner can't agree on the big ticket items, consider if you'd be better off with someone else, or on your own.

Really? That last bullet, is that so terrible? And in case you are wondering, I was able to keep my house, my pension, and some of my savings – I just have to keep working until I'm eighty to pay off my supersize mortgage. Thankfully, I love my job. More importantly, I removed someone from my life who, even though I loved him, was causing me great anxiety, grief, and pain. Now I have hope, new love, and new possibilities.

So. I'd say the fight was worth it.

[#]

My fight is over. Now, it is up to you, both of you, whoever you are - Wendy and Peter or Wendell and Petra or Wendy and Petra and Wendell and Peter - to craft the deal that you both can live with. Not just for today, when you're all soaked in lust and pheromones and excitement, but tomorrow too, when the rose is not so rosy, you're waking up to the same old face on the pillow, and after you've hit a few bumps along the road to happily ever.

And that's another thing that's bugging me. Relationships

are *hard*. All of them, every single one. After the first year or two, after the mad sex and soulmate buzz has started to ease into the more mature realm of compromise, mutual support, recognition of flaws and needs, gives and takes, disappointments and turn offs, sometimes there are going to be days when you think, *oh my God, why am I with you?* But no one in Hollywood or on TikTok is telling us this because there, it's all about the Big Kiss and the ride off into the sunset. So when we hit the first bump, turnoff, disappointment, whiff of bad breath, poor choice of shoes, whatever, we think, *Whoa, maybe this dude (or dudette) ain't our cup of tea after all.* And then many of us, sadly, cut and run, before turning up at a family lawyer's office.

I still have hope for love. Real love. Mature love. Where you see the person for who they truly are, and not through pheromone-infused glasses, and love them anyway. And they you. But staying in a relationship with anyone—a friend, a co-worker, a parent, a sibling, a company, a lover, a spouse, a dog, a cat, or a horse—is a choice. All this soulmate hoo-hah is for Hollywood. For real people living real lives, it's a choice they have to make every day. Sometimes it's easy; most of the time it's not. Relationships are hard work, not for the faint-hearted, or the Peter and Petra Pans of the world, that's for sure. But even for the rest of us it's hard to know when you should stay and fight for it, and when you should walk away. Just don't be a flake. Don't make promises you can't keep and break hearts that are trying to mend. There's another person involved here and they don't deserve that.

I still believe a well-written cohab can save a relationship, even one between a Wendy/Wendell and a Peter/Petra, as long as one of you isn't also a Dick. And yes, even though there may be some things more important to you than not getting fleeced - don't ask me for examples, I'm a Capricorn - no one wants to feel like they put their heart and soul out there and got scammed anyway. I don't care what sign you are.

Bonus Tip: Get Perspective.

Okay, despite all the pain and anger I've been going on about, let's take a trip to Mars and look down at the situation from there. From where we can see Earth convulsing from climate change, mass extinction, starvation, disease, and senseless war. Just because the ex broke our heart and took some of our money, is this the end of the world as we know it? We'll get there due to bigger crimes than your Dick/Dickette is capable of. So, let's take a deep breath and get some perspective. Because at some point, win or lose, we all have to cut our losses, and get on with the rest of our lives.

> *"Live every day as your last because one of these days it will be."*
> —Jonathan Swift

But before any of that happens...

Here's Another Recap

What I learned about the Law:

It has evolved to protect the lower-earning spouse, regardless of the circumstances.

It's always changing, but not always keeping up with the times.

It is does not favour the partner with the job and the assets.

It doesn't protect us from empty promises.

It doesn't protect our boundaries (only we can do that).

It likes to split things down the middle, no questions asked, unless you have an agreement that says otherwise.

It upholds agreements that are precise and explicit, but not if they are deemed unfair.

It allows judges to uphold valid contracts, but validity is in the eye of the beholder.

It favours deadbeats.

If your lawyer isn't on the same page as you, you're going into a fight with one hand tied behind your back.

Everyone, including the lawyers, will do everything and anything to stay out of a family law court room.

Know when to fight back, and when to walk away - from your ex, your lawyer, and the battlefield.

What I learned about Love:

That's it's really hard to find.

But not worth being so desperate for it that we are our own undoing.

The sooner we stand up for our boundaries, the safer we'll be, whether or not the relationship survives.

No one can be as cruel as someone who once said they love you.

The breakup will be as painful, and as costly, as the relationship.

Forget about the gaga - if you don't trust and respect them, don't let them move in.

Don't fall in love with a deadbeat.

Love yourself first and best before trying to love someone else.

Don't let anyone call you petty.

Never forget about Fido – who will always love you first and best.

What I learned about Cohab Agreements

Start with your values and your boundaries, both yours and your partners.

Writing one can help you and your partner figure out if you both trust and respect each other enough to live together.

You can agree to divide property and debt any way you like.

Anything goes as long as you can prove it, and the courts can find it "reasonable".

Make sure it considers plans and savings for the future.

Only agree to divide stuff, including your income, if it makes sense for your relationship.

You can ask that your partner:

Keep a job, to not become financially dependent on you.

Waive spousal support under certain circumstances, such as re-partnering.

Keep their own pension or put equivalent savings into an RRSP.

If the partner refuses to, or can't, save for retirement, that they waive their rights to your pension or to agree to an unequal split.

They sign a waiver on spousal support, with the provision to make changes as the family changes or grows.

Future-proof the heck out of it - consider *all* aspects of cohabitation and separation, in life and in death.

A promise is a promise, but only if it's in writing.

CONCLUSION: DARN YOUR WOOL

Say what you will, I love William Shatner (even more than I love Jonathan Swift). My dad did too. When asked if he was sad about his fourth marriage ending, Shatner said, "I'm almost ninety years old, nothing makes me sad," or something like that. I'm not sure those are words to live by, but there's something galvanizing about the idea that at some point you grow up too much to give a fig flying through the air a second glance.

At the end of the day, each of us knits our own sweater. And we often end up with who we end up with because of some shit in our past that didn't get properly dealt with. Now, too many years later, I recognize that many of my relationship choices, including a Peter Pan who took advantage of me, were reflections of unresolved issues with my mother, the one for whom I was never good enough, and my younger brother, the Lost Boy I could never rescue. At the same time, I recognize that those labels are not something those people deserved, or even earned. My mother overcame the horrors of war, being orphaned, being lost, and became a nurse, a wife, and a mother. A mother who taught us to stand up for what we felt was right and what we believed in. My brother is now less lost than me, as the father of three beautiful boys and who works in environmental science. We have to take responsibility for our own vulnerabilities and mistakes, so that we can grow beyond them.

It seems to me that sometimes we accept something in our life to atone for things we feel guilty about. I had accepted my ex-husband's pension because I was scared, unemployed, and angry that he'd ditched me, but it plagued me with guilt. I felt that I should never have put myself in a position where I needed someone else's pension: don't take what you don't earn, my mother reminded me, on more than one occasion. I totally agree with her—she's one of the most principled people I know—but I was scared. I was over forty. I was unemployed. A cull ewe. Family law said I could take it so I did. And I hated myself for it. So, what happened ten years later? Dick did the same thing to me.

I was a sitting duck for Dick, in so many ways. He opened the windows to the natural, wild, world I had turned my back on. He was a Lost Boy I could rescue. He was the one person who loved me unconditionally, the way my mother never could, or so he pretended, in order to get what he wanted. The world is full of victims and predators, people with gaping wounds and sagging baggage, and those who know just how to pick them up, dust them off, and use them for their own purposes. Sugar daddies and mommas, artful dodgers and pimps, Peters and Dicks, have refined this skill across the ages. I often wonder how these people justify their actions to themselves after they pluck some vulnerable waif off the street and put them to work for their own gain. I guess they too are products of their own dysfunction.

I mentioned that I ride horses, or try to - it's a tricky business and I don't bounce very well anymore. During one session, after I'd ranted about some slight by some guy I was dating, my riding instructor told me that, generally speaking, people are just doing the best they can given who they are and with whatever tools they have been given to navigate this life. Riding instructors have to cope with large, complex, sensitive, and highly reactive animals being ridden by anxious, demanding, fearful, and sometimes spoiled princesses, and so many of these fine humans have developed tremendous insight and intuition into both species. As a matter of survival. So what he said really stuck with me, and I try to remember it whenever I get too upset over Dick's money grab.

My Dick may have been a narcissistic Peter Pan who bent the truth to get what he wanted, but I don't believe he was a sociopath. He was doing the best he could with what he had —great hair, a sense of humour, appendages he knew how to use, a possible personality disorder and maybe even a frontal lobe injury. When he went after me for money he didn't earn, I don't think he did it to spite or injure me. I don't think he gave a flying fig about how it affected me. All he knew was that he didn't have a job or a house and he was getting old and the law said he could take stuff from me so he did. Believe it or not, I'm not really all that mad at him anymore. I'm madder at the system that allows people to do what Dick did to me, at a system that not only allows for deadbeat-ism but actually encourages it! Because all you have to do is shack up with somebody with a lot more money than you, sit around and do nothing, and then roll out the door with a bag full of money. And if they don't have a cohab with you, there's nothing they can do about it. It's not like winning the lottery—it's a sure thing! So if you're someone with a sense of entitlement and not a heck of a lot of integrity, why wouldn't you give that a go?

That means that it's up to those of us who *do* work for what we have, who *do* have a sense of integrity and fairness, to protect ourselves. Family law isn't going to. It can't. Because it was designed to protect the stay-at-home spouses and the newlyweds who built everything they have together, not the Wendys and Wendells of the world, who despite their best intentions end up in bed with a Peter-turned-Dick or a Petra-turned-Dickette. It's also up to us to *not* be a victim - not of the vagaries of family law, not of the Chancers looking for an easy ride, and not of the unresolved issues of our pasts.

But there's another way to look at this.

Dick and I eventually settled our dispute, and he got way more than he should have, according to me, my lawyer, my family, friends, partner, etc. But what if Dick really did love me, at least to the best of his ability? What if he really was doing his best, with the tools that he had, contributed what he could, committed as best he could, but it was never good enough? What if a frontal lobe injury or alexithymia prevented him from getting the job I thought he would but couldn't? What if the depression and fears I believe he suffered from handcuffed him to perpetual underachievement? What if I decided I didn't want to be saddled with "a loser" who couldn't perform at the level I held for myself, didn't want to get stuck with someone who might become mentally disabled, and what if I waited for the best opportunity, when house prices had fallen and I could afford the risk, to throw him out in the middle of winter, jobless, with little more than the clothes on his back and his camper van? Who's the C U Next Tuesday now?

This is no doubt close to the narrative Dick told himself, his lawyer, his family, and his friends as he justified his actions. In Dick's reality, the money he got is paltry compensation for the time we spent together and certainly not enough to give him the life he felt he'd earned.

Which means there's my story, Dick's story, and the law. But in the murkiness of our narratives, pain, injuries, disappointments, and the damage we do to people we once loved, the law can't find the truth. Perhaps it lies somewhere between Dick's story and mine, but who knows where? That's why justice is blind. Why it *has* to be. And why we need to protect ourselves by knowing ourselves because no one else—and certainly not family law—can do it for us.

"Honor is a harder master than the law."
—Mark Twain

So, there you have it. After almost three years, thirteen lawyers, three judges, three court appearances, and two court orders, I ran out of battles to fight. At midnight the night before my last trial date, my lawyer called me to say we were now a few thousand dollars apart and that tomorrow I was probably going to lose. I finally had to accept that family law, and Dick, were going to have their way with me, no matter how hard I fought for what I thought was fair. And so I settled, giving Dick way more money than he deserved but also way less than he was going for, fulfilling the old adage that there are no winners in family law, only rich lawyers. Not that I begrudge the lawyers who worked with me and advised me—they were all honourable, honest, and hard-working: the three things Dick was not. How ironic is that?

And after my fight was over, I realized something. Something that eluded me in my rage, in all my battles, something really, really important…

That my heart would always be broken. Even if I had "won" my battle against Dick and he got what he deserved, which was nothing more than a kick in the pants, I would still be heartbroken. Not in an irreparable, "my life is over" kind of way, but like a wound that leaves a scar that will never completely disappear.

Dick presented the fantasy that I had finally found my soulmate, my forever man, my Hollywood happily ever after guy. But it was an act, a facade, a lie he could only maintain long enough for me to screw myself over. When the emotional and financial abuse started, I was so desperate to hold on to my dream of what my future was supposed to be, with my perfectly wonderful soulmate, that I let that abuse go on for years. I turned away, from the truth, from my friends, and from myself, in a desperate battle with the construct of what I thought my life was supposed to be, the one I had planned and dreamed of since I was a little girl, the one I had written about in countless romance novels and screenplays, always with a heartfelt cause of saving what was about to be lost—the rainforest, the frogs, the wolves, the tigers, the killer whales, the last Inca fortress, you name it—and always with a Lost Boy falling for a woman who was strong enough to save them both. A woman who was, despite different hair and body types, essentially me. I had given up on Dick years ago, I had seen what he really was long before the day we finally broke up. But I hadn't given up on my dream. Now I had to face the fact that my dream was the delusion of someone who, just like Dick, was a middle-aged child. A little-girl princess who never grew up, holding on to an illusion fed by fairy tales, social media, and ego. Then I decided that, at the ripe old age of—you go ahead and guess—it was time to finally grow the hell up.

The VBP who helped me through this told me, long before I was ready to hear it, that I had the power to turn this slog of abuse and legalized theft into a journey of growth and self-discovery... Ya, okay, I just threw up a little bit too, but it's true. I learned a whole whack of stuff about myself that I never knew. Win or lose at family law, it can be the same for you. The VBP also recommended I read a book called *Spiritual Divorce: Divorce as a Catalyst for an Extraordinary Life*, by the extraordinary Debbie Ford.[103] It's a wonderful, comforting, inspiring book that I recommend for anyone going through the pain of a shattered heart and broken dreams, and its core message is this: that you are exactly where you need to be, right now, right here, in the middle of this shit-show (I'm paraphrasing) because through it you will recognize your own shortcomings in order to become who you were meant to be, and live the life you were meant to live.

Earlier in the book, I talked about how we fall for someone who opens our hidden boxes, fills the holes in our broken souls. For some of you, your ex gave you beautiful children that would not have existed were it not for this karmic, transitory union. Perhaps through your ex, you discovered, or re-discovered, a desire to sing, or paint, or build. Dick, through his love of adventure and wilderness, revealed to me my buried environmentalist, which sparked the passion and vocation I currently have.

These people, our Dicks and Dickettes, even though they don't mean to, teach us important lessons about ourselves, reveal drives and desires we have long tucked away. They give us important, although unintentional, gifts, even as they hurt us. It's up to us to take all that pain, roll it up into a tight, hot ball, and then release it as a beacon of energy that lights up our new path.

My dad fought this fight as hard as I did. He was very ill, but despite his pain and frailty he was with me every step of the way. Almost to the end. Dad always told me: "Pay attention to what people do, not what they say. Words come cheap, but actions count." I wish I'd remembered that before I let Dick move in with me. I would have saved myself, and my family, a lot of grief. He was the one who recognized Dick for what he was right from the get-go but held his tongue because he saw how crazy I was about the guy. But he stopped holding back the moment Dick went after me for money.

Dad encouraged me to keep fighting for what I thought was right for as long as I could, because he knew that's what I could live with, whatever the outcome. When it became apparent that we were up against a system that was punitive toward people like me, unable to pivot away from awarding a narcissistic predator because of the ways its laws are written, Dad told me I had to write this book.

At first, I was wary. "I'm not a lawyer," I said. "Isn't it rather audacious, impudent even, of me to write something like this?" But Dad kept asking when I was going to write about this, and eventually, after the third or fourth time he brought it up, I said, "You know what, maybe I will. Maybe if I just write about what happened to me it'll save someone else from going through what I did. If that happens, then maybe all the shit Dick put me through will have been worth it."

"Aw, screw that," Dad bellowed. "Write a goddamn bestseller and then *you* go make some money off that fucker for a change." Like I said, Dad had stopped holding back.

My dad died before a final settlement was reached. During his last weeks, when his pain and illness got too much for him to bear, I told him it was okay to let go, that we, his family, would be okay, if he had to go. I never said it out loud; my dad was a fighter and I didn't want to take that away from him. But one day he said to me, "I'm really tired and I've got to go," and then he did. Now his big lovely spirit is free from the crumpled body that betrayed him. And I hope he knows that it all turned out okay, despite Dick's fuckery and a legal system that favours deadbeats. I hope he knows that I finally wrote this book, and that, after all the things he taught me—like how to fight for what you believe in—he taught me one last, most important lesson:

If you don't let go, you can't be free.

I now believe I had to go through this relationship with Dick, with all its love and larceny, to discover who I really was and what I could possibly contribute to this planet. And so, I let my Lost Boy go, along with some of my money and, more importantly, my foolish fairy-tale dreams. And I hugged my broken heart because now, just like when you break a bone, it was stronger. Stronger than ever before, and it even felt a bit bigger too. Not in a Medical Alert kind of way but in a way that lets a lot more people in, including the man I love today. I'm glad I met him when I did, after I went through all of this, after I grew up... because he's an adult who deserves an adult relationship with someone capable of loving him for real, in the real world. That's what this journey did for me. It made me worthy of the love I finally found. But more than that, I found me.

I hope the same for you. I've been bugging you to read your family law statutes, but now I implore you to read books like those by Debbie Ford, Neil Pasricha, Harriet Lerner, anything about saving yourself from a toxic relationship. This happened to you because you have not finished your self-discovery. This disappointment, this heartbreak, this agony, this family law freak-show is your chance. Don't waste it.

> *"Regret is the worst human emotion. If you took another road, you might have fallen off a cliff."*—William Shatner

Speaking of dreams, I mentioned that during my relationship with Dick I'd have some really strange ones—nightmares really. Off we'd go in his camper van on some adventure; he'd drive and I would be enjoying the ride so much I hadn't paid attention to where he was taking me. We'd stop somewhere and he'd tell me how much he loved me, how beautiful I was, how we were destined to be together, and I'd be filled to the brim with love and happiness. But suddenly he'd grow cold and turn away, sometimes to talk to another woman, or to disappear down the street or behind a door. I'd try to talk to him, to find him again, or beg for an explanation for his change of heart. I'd desperately try, urgently search, but would get nowhere. Instead, I'd realize that I was now lost in some dark, strange, and twisted landscape. None of my maps or phone apps made sense, so I couldn't figure out where I was. Utterly lost. And I'd let him take me there, unable to find my way back. Terrified, I'd wake up to find him sleeping next to me. It was all I could do to not sob out loud in relief.

What does it mean? I'm just guessing, but I think it's about loving someone so much that you lose yourself, let yourself be taken to some place where you don't even recognize yourself, and don't know how to find your way back to who and what you once were. I think it's also a warning: that it's better to be alone than in a relationship with someone who does that to you. Don't get me wrong, I fully appreciate all the challenges of being alone, believe me—the bad dates, the single glass of wine, only one set of hands, the loneliness, even fear, especially at night, and not having that shoulder to cry on after a crappy day. Get a dog or, even better, a horse (big shoulder to cry on and they never tell you to get over yourself, just to pass the carrots). But even without a dog or a horse, it's still better to be alone than with someone who emotionally and financially drains you. Someone who is emotionally draining but financially supportive of your life, your hopes, your future together—maybe you can live with that. Someone who is financially dependent but fills you up emotionally, stands by you no matter what, makes you feel good about yourself just the way you are—you can probably live with that too. But emotionally *and* financially draining? Don't do it.

Years later, now that the legal dust has settled and my bank accounts are smaller, I sometimes have that same dream. I haven't seen or spoken to Dick in years, but that dream haunts me still. The place may be different but Dick's actions are the same, and I'm always left in some dark and twisted place, trying to find my way home and I can't... But now, when I wake up to see that he's *not* sleeping next to me, I heave a great sigh of relief.

I think I still have that dream to remind me not to dial Dick's number, not that I ever would. Swear.

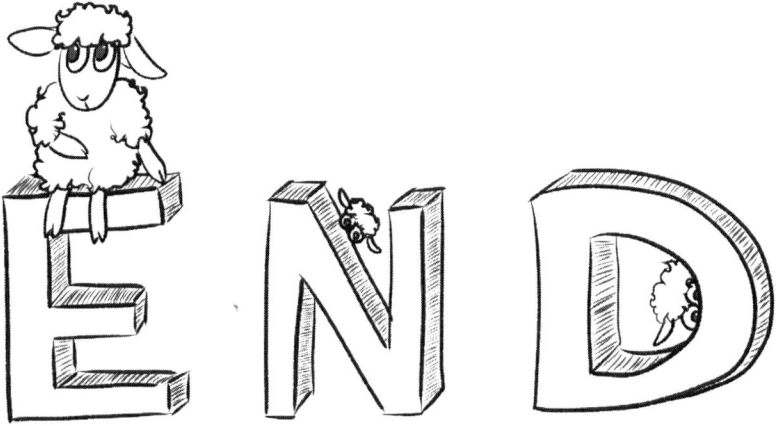

APPENDICES

APPENDIX 1: MY LEGAL JOURNEY

This is a quick chronology of what happened to me, just in case you got lost in some of my yarn:

After I separate from my husband of almost twenty years, Lawyer No. 1 works out my terms of separation. My soon-to-be ex-husband is generous. I feel guilty.

A year later, I meet Dick online as BC's *Family Law Act (FLA)* is amended to equalize the rights of common-law spouses with the rights of married ones. And I buy a house.

That summer, Dick moves into my house and Lawyer No. 1 starts drafting our cohabitation agreement, trying to navigate the new *FLA.*

The following spring, Lawyer No. 1 leaves the province. Lawyer No. 2 takes over Lawyer No. 1's cases and tries to warn me about my exposure in the CA. But I sign it anyway.

A few months later, Dick quits his full-time job and cashes in his divisible pension. He does not share it with me.

Meanwhile, I secure a full-time job plus pension. Now, Dick works only part-time, some of the time, and does not contribute to a divisible pension, only to his savings and condo which I had agreed would not be divided. He tells me he can't afford to maintain his obligations under the CA but still wants to be able to cash in on it. He also reneges on a promise to sell his condo and invest in the house.

Two years before breakup, Dick has reneged on all his commitments and refuses to change the CA, still intending to cash in on my divisible pension and the house. I tell him to leave and we break up. I consult with Lawyer No. 3, who tells me about a client of his in a similar situation who just lost her house. For the first time I fully realize how dangerous the *FLA* is for someone like me.

Later that same year, Dick and I reconcile on the condition we amend our CA. Lawyer No. 3 recommends Lawyer No. 4, a junior associate at Lawyer No. 3's firm with a focus on collaborative process, to draft the amendment. Dick and I are reconciling, right? So I want to collaborate, right?

Springtime breakup: After years of operating under the new agreement, Dick announces he'll never sign it and I kick him out, for good this time. Lawyer No. 4 thinks I have a shot at settling under the unsigned amendment anyway so I hire him to get it done. Dick files a family law claim and puts a lien on my house.

The summer after the breakup, as Dick drags me through the family law process, I consult Lawyer No. 5 for a second opinion while still contracted with Lawyer No. 4. No. 5 is from the same firm as Nos. 1 & 2 and tells me how the original CA was supposed to work: dividing the increased value in the house if Dick contributes to its expenses. But the expense clause is too tenuously connected to the division clause, so Dick's lawyer wriggles him out of it.

Later that same summer, I get my pension evaluated, which has skyrocketed in value due to low interest rates. Still contracted with Lawyer No. 4, he now tells me that he agrees with Dick's lawyer that I'll likely have to settle under the original CA, which is, aside from the "no spousal support" clause, essentially the same as the new *FLA*. So I'm probably flocked.

That fall, Lawyer No. 4 throws me under the bus (or so it felt) during a JCC[104] by not prepping me about what could happen and not speaking up when Dick's shark lawyer gets the judge to see things Dick's way. I refuse to mediate so the judge sets trial.

Frazzled, I call Lawyer No. 6, who has a reputation as a strategic litigator. No. 6 tells me that I was crazy to sign that CA but temporary insanity will not get me out of it. Thank you, that will be $700, please.

One year after breakup, I get trial adjourned due to work commitments, on the condition I agree to a mediation after all. The new trial is set for a few months later. *Oh good,* I think, *lots of time to build my case* (ha!).

Later that spring, I consult with a civil litigator, Lawyer No. 7, about both my agreements, who assures me that both are valid contracts, but only if I can prove the unsigned one, which is essentially the same thing Lawyer No. 4 told me, just not as nicely.

Dick's shark is pushing for the mediation I agreed to. I call a very senior lawyer (No. 8) to ask for advice. She tells me that collaborative law is a bunch of bunk in contentious cases such as mine where there has been some form of abuse, emotional or otherwise. I try to get out of the mediation, but the lawyers have worked out a deal over it (we agree to adjourn, you mediate) so I'm stuck with it.

Later that year, I consult with another civil litigator (Lawyer No. 9) about whether I can sue Dick in civil court for misrepresentation (also known as fraud, but this sounds nicer) and breach of contract, regardless of what happens at family court. Sadly, No. 9 tells me that I am in the purview of family law and so the bucks (all of them) stop there. Plus, he tells me, so horribly succinctly, that family law favours deadbeats so you are indeed flocked. *Have you met Lawyer No. 4?* I want to ask him. *If not, I'll arrange an intro. You guys will get along great!*

A few months later, mediation costs me $6,000 to confirm for me that Dick is indeed a greedy asshole. But, hey, at least I can say to the judge that I tried it. At this point, Lawyer No. 4 seems to be on board that we are headed for a courtroom. So I spend thousands more dollars getting ready for trial: witnesses, documentation, planning, and, of course, discovery.

Around this time, I'm starting to listen to my gut that No. 4 and I are not on the same page. Lawyer No. 10 is a seasoned attorney with a reputation of being a barracuda, but she's also retiring and so can't take my case, so I hire her as a shadow lawyer, to review advice and strategy from No. 4 and make sure we are on track. Now I'm paying two lawyers at the same time for essentially the same advice, but No. 10 does give me some ideas on how to fight back (see Chapter 11: "Ram versus Lamb").

Two years after breakup, mid-summer: Heading toward trial, Dick forces a re-evaluation of my house, which has increased in value by over 30% over the course of our legal battle, while low interest rates have fattened the divisible portion of my pension. Gulp.

Two years after breakup, late summer, just two days before trial, No. 4 has a stress-related collapse and so we must adjourn until the following spring. Oh well, as long as No. 4 is okay (which he was, thankfully, a few days later).

That fall, I amend my counterclaim to Dick's family law claim to include upholding the amended CA on the basis of section 92 and claiming unjust enrichment due to his failure to meet his CA obligations. Dick fights back with: Well, if you're calling the CA into question, then I want the full-meal deal, including spousal support (you could say the dude had no pride, but I too sunk to a new low, later on) and division of the *entire* house, not just the increase in value, because it's family property. It's not, but still... Gulp.

That winter, Dick's shark asks for another discovery, where she rakes me over the coals to demonstrate (to who: me or my lawyer?) that the second agreement is not an agreement at all but rather an agreement to agree, which doesn't stand up in court (where the flock was the preparation, Lawyer No. 4?).

Three years after breakup: Once again, it's days before trial. Lawyer No. 4 is now quite convinced that calm, cool Dick with a signed CA in hand will win the day, despite all my evidence about the amendment and the thousands of dollars I spent collecting it. I'm a sobbing, stressed-out mess when Lawyer No.

3 strolls in to tell me the story about the woman who lost half her house to a man who beat her.

That night, Dick's lawyer sends over an offer that includes penalties if I don't accept it. Lawyer No. 4 says I'm crazy if I don't accept this deal. I should have read the echo, but my dad was very sick at this point, on top of everything else, and so I crack under the pressure and say okay after too many glasses of Pinot Noir (not again!).

A day later, I realize my mistake. I attempt to use deficiencies, like omitting the removal of the lien on my house, and other technicalities to overturn the deal, saying it's actually just an agreement to agree. Dick launches an application to force me to honour it. I find myself wondering if he appreciates the irony.

Later that spring, during the application, Lawyer No. 4 throws me under the bus again, or so it felt, by siding with Dick's lawyer about the settlement deal. Despite this, the judge grants me a summary trial to determine the validity of the "deal."

I end my relationship with Lawyer No. 4.

My dad dies.

While grieving my father, I desperately search for a new lawyer. After Lawyer No. 10 turns me down again, I hire Lawyer No. 12 and No. 13's firm (after consulting with Lawyer No. 11) to handle the summary trial and final negotiations. No. 12 wins our application to delay trial until the summer but tells me we need to maintain control through negotiation rather than trial because you never know what the hell a judge is going to do or say. My dreams of vindication at trial are really starting to fade now!

It's now three and a half years after breakup and that summer, after months of back and forth, both Nos. 12 and 13 tell me they can't find a big enough loophole to give them confidence to go to trial to try to overturn the separation "agreement" arrived at a few months prior. The only thing I can do is plead duress due to my father's sickness and death. I let them. We send an affidavit to Dick's shark. It's a new low for me: leveraging my dad's suffering to get out of a deal.

But it doesn't get that far. Rising interest rates turn the tide. Instead of dividing my pension, Lawyer No. 13 offers Dick a chunk of my RRSPs, at a discount, due to my pension's falling value with higher interest rates. We go back and forth over what my pension is worth now, haggling over a few thousand dollars until midnight before trial.

"Family law is fucked up," Lawyer No. 13 tells me, her voice cracking. We are both so tired. It is now almost four years after the break up and it's been hours of Dick continually saying he won't negotiate before coming back "one more time." It's obvious how badly he wants to avoid the trial, but then she says, "Don't let it fuck you up any more than it already has." And I say, finally, "Okay. Done. I'm done. Let Dick have his pound of flesh. I have better things to do… like honour my father."

And write this book!

APPENDIX 2: QUICK LINKS TO FAMILY LAW IN YOUR JURISDICTION

Researching this book led me to family law statutes and informational websites across the country and the border. Here are some salient links all in one helpful place.

Canada
Divorce Act: https://laws-lois.justice.gc.ca/eng/acts/d-3.4/
Changes to the Divorce Act: https://www.justice.gc.ca/eng/fl-df/cfl-mdf/index.html
Which provinces recognize common-law marriage: https://jurigo.ca/en/common-law-partner/

British Columbia
FLA: https://www2.gov.bc.ca/gov/content/life-events/divorce/family-justice/the-family-law-act
https://family.legalaid.bc.ca/
Supreme Court & Family Law: https://supremecourtbc.ca/family-law
Cohab agreements: https://www.lawdepot.ca/contracts/cohabitation-agreement/
Financial Disclosure: https://family.legalaid.bc.ca/finances-support/child-spousal-support/what-financial-disclosure
BC provides a website on the various steps, courts, and issues to be considered when separating: www.howtoseparate.ca

Pensions and Other Benefits: https://family.legalaid.bc.ca/finances-support/property-debt/dividing-pensions-and-other-benefits-after-you-separate

Alberta
FLA: https://open.alberta.ca/publications/f04p5
https://www.alberta.ca/family-law-legislation

Ontario
FLA: https://www.ontario.ca/laws/statute/90f03
Cohab Agreements: https://divorcethesmartway.ca/wiki/cohabitation-agreement-ontario/
Differences between provinces: https://richtertriallaw.com/2018/08/18/ontario-vs-british-columbia-where-you-file-for-divorce-matters/

Quebec
https://www.quebec.ca/en/family-and-support-for-individuals/separation-divorce
Family law within the civil code of Quebec: https://www.legisquebec.gouv.qc.ca/en/tdm/cs/CCQ-1991
https://familylawyer.zone/family-law-quebec/
Differences between provinces: https://www.ylaw.ca/blog/differences-between-quebec-family-law-and-bc-divorce-law/

United States:
Federal: https://www.state.gov/family-law/
US Case Law: https://law.justia.com/cases/
https://www.law.cornell.edu/wex/family_court
Justia can link you to the family law code and statue in your state. Here's California, for example: https://law.justia.com/codes/california/2022/code-fam/ where common-law marriage is not recognized, versus Colorado, which does: https://law.justia.com/codes/colorado/2022/title-14/ at least as of this writing.

APPENDIX 3: THE COHAB I WISH I HAD WRITTEN

My ideal cohab may not be your ideal cohab because you and I have a different set of boundaries and a different set of circumstances. And, I hope for your sake, you also have a different Dick/Dickette. *So I'm not offering this as a template.* You need to take your and your partner's boundaries and circumstances to a good lawyer to get a cohab that's right for you. But having said all of that, I believe that if my cohabitation agreement with Dick had been written like this, one of two things would have happened:

> I would not have been so stressed and angry by my boundaries being crossed all the time, and maybe Dick and I would have found some kind of equilibrium where our relationship didn't devolve into a pile of shit. Or:

> Dick would have skedaddled right away in search of more gullible prey.

Most of the time I suspect the second outcome to be much more likely, but hey, sometimes people surprise you. As I wrote earlier, people evolve within relationships and relationships evolve because of the people within them. If I'd had the cohab I'm sharing with you now, would I have still turned into an anxious, overweight Seven-Year Bitch? I don't think so - I'm a little thinner now, for one thing, and a lot less angry. Is it possible Dick wouldn't have turned into such a Dick? Only he knows the answer to that one.

Speaking of templates, there are quite a few good ones out there now. Some may be a bit too cut and dried for those of us who are hoping for, and being promised, an equal partnership. But I still recommend you check them out to get a baseline:

> https://dialalaw.peopleslawschool.ca/marriage-agreements/
> https://www.lawdepot.ca/contracts/cohabitation-agreement
> https://www.findlaw.com/family/living-together/sample-cohabitation-agreement.html

These templates are written for Canadian law but the basic principles can transfer to other common law (but not civil law!) jurisdictions.

But, please, please, please read this caveat: for families who have decided that one partner forgoes employment and financial gain to be a stay-at-home caregiver of anyone, be they children, parents, or a herd of llamas. If you are one of those people, family law WAS written to protect you, so use it.

But for the rest of us, here it is, the cohab agreement I *wish* I had signed with Dick, based on my boundaries, my circumstances, my sense of fairness and justice, and where Dick was at when he moved in with me. Just in case it helps and inspires you to write yours. And if does, great! That's why I wrote this bloody book. But *please*, it's just a starting point! And you should still get legal advice. After you have draft terms, find a lawyer you trust and who is willing to communicate with you, who is willing to fight for your boundaries and sense of fairness, and then let them do their job, which is to make sure your cohab is right for you, the relationship you have with your partner, and, most important of all, your future.

This Agreement Dated The _____ Day Of _____, Y_____.

BETWEEN:
Cinoma Bronhill
(hereinafter referred to as "CB")
OF THE FIRST PART
AND:
DICK PETER CHANCER
(hereinafter referred to as "Dick")
OF THE SECOND PART
WHEREAS:
A. The parties commenced cohabitation on DDMMYY and intend to continue cohabiting in a marriage-like relationship in the future;
B. Dick's date of birth is DDMMYY. Dick is trained in [this] and [that], currently working for [name of employer] as of DDMMYY. His line 150 income in DDMMYY was [not very much]. His DDMMYY earnings from employment were approximately [a lot more].
C. CB's date of birth is DDMMYY. CB is trained in [something pretty good] and has worked in several different capacities,

including as [some rather cool stuff]. CB's earnings fluctuate substantially. Her line 150 income in DDMMYY was [not too shabby]. Her DDMMYY earnings from employment were approximately [could have been better] with some additional investment income.

D. Dick has been divorced from his former wife since DDMMYY. Dick and his former wife entered into a Separation Agreement dated DDMMYY (attached hereto as Schedule "A") and Dick warrants and represents that all transactions/obligations under that agreement have concluded.

E. CB has been living separate and apart from her former husband since DDMMYY and was divorced by order of the court made DDMMYY. CB and her former husband entered into a Separation Agreement dated DDMMYY and Amending Agreement dated DDMMYY, which are attached hereto as Schedules[105] "B" and "C," respectively.

F. Neither CB nor Dick has children from previous relationships. This Agreement applies whether or not they have children together.

G. CB is the registered owner of [a house in Vancouver], more particularly known and described as:

PID XXX-XXX-XXX, etc., (the "House")

H. CB purchased the House on DDMMYY for [a lot of money]. It is encumbered by a [bank] mortgage in the initial amount of [even more money]. CB paid the balance of the purchase price from personal funds that were her sole property. It is anticipated that the parties will reside in the House for a period of time, and that CB intends to upgrade the property.

I. CB's personal assets ("CB's Assets"), liabilities ("CB's Liabilities"), and Pets as at DDMMYY are set out in Schedule "D."

J. As a result of her previous marriage CB has a right to an interest in a [provincial] pension plan as a limited member, arising from her interest in [former husband]'s pension during their marriage ("CB's Pension"). It is possible that CB will have the opportunity to transfer CB's Pension to a locked-in RRSP in the event that [former husband] terminates his employment with [his company] and also transfers his portion of his pension to a locked-in RRSP.

K. Dick is the registered owner of [a condo in Vancouver], more particularly known and described as:

PID YYY-YYY-YYY, etc. (the "Condo")

L. Dick purchased the Condo in DDMMYY. Its DDMMYY BC Assessment Value, which the parties agree to be its fair market value, is [less than half the house]. It is presently encumbered by a [name of bank] mortgage in the approximate amount of [a small fraction of my mortgage]. It is currently rented to tenants and is expected to incur capital gains tax upon disposition for the portion of time that it was not Dick's primary residence.

M. Dick's personal assets ("Dick's Assets") and liabilities ("Dick's Liabilities") as at DDMMYY are set out in Schedule "E."

N. Dick has a right to an interest in a pension plan as a result of his employment with [Employer], where he worked from DDMMYY to DDMMYY, from which he anticipates receiving $XXXX/month plus a Y% per annum cost of living increase if commenced at his age 60. With his job with [Another Employer], Dick has and will continue to accumulate an interest in this second pension plan.

O. CB and Dick do not currently have joint assets.

P. CB has provided Dick full and true information for the purposes of reaching this Agreement.

Q. Dick has provided CB full and true information for the purposes of reaching this Agreement.

R. The parties are both satisfied with the knowledge and disclosure each has of the other's assets and liabilities and neither of them requires further or better particulars of the assets and liabilities of the other for the purposes of this Agreement.

S. Dick and CB separately intend this Agreement to be:

    (a) the final settlement of their respective rights in or to the property of the other and the property held by them jointly;

    (b) a full release of any right, interest, or claim which either party may have upon the property of the other;

(c) a settlement with respect to spousal support.

NOW THEREFORE IN CONSIDERATION OF THE PREMISES AND MUTUAL COVENANTS CONTAINED IN THIS AGREEMENT, THE PARTIES AGREE AS FOLLOWS:

CONFIRMATION OF RECITALS[106]

1. CB warrants and represents that the statements of fact contained in recitals [relevant to CB] are accurate and true.

2. Dick warrants and represents that the statements of fact contained in recitals [relevant to Dick] are accurate and true.

PURPOSE OF AGREEMENT (or INTENTION OF THE PARTIES)

3. This Agreement governs the parties' relationship whether or not they are "spouses" as defined in the *Family Law Act*. This Agreement will remain in effect during their relationship (including marriage if they marry) and after it ends.

4. If and when the parties become spouses within the meaning of the *Family Law Act*, this Agreement is intended to be a property agreement within the meaning of section 92 of the *Family Law Act*.

5. The parties understand, which understanding is one of the fundamental premises of this Agreement, that:

(a) The acquisition of each party's assets has not been and will not be as a result of the joint efforts of the parties nor as a result of their relationship,

(b) Each party's assets may continue to increase substantially in value, or may decrease substantially in value, and,

(c) Each party should be free to make the estate planning decisions that each of them deems fit;

(d) This Agreement must not impair CB's ability to fulfill her obligations to [her ex-husband] as set out in Schedules "A" and "B," which obligations pre-exist this Agreement and are known to both parties in entering into this Agreement.

6. As a result of the understanding reflected in the foregoing

paragraph, the parties intend by this Agreement to provide that, except as otherwise provided in this Agreement, CB's assets are protected from any claim by Dick, and Dick's assets are protected from any claim by CB, in the event their relationship breaks down, regardless of:

(a) Any increase or decrease in value of a party's assets during the course of the parties' relationship;

(b) The duration of the parties' relationship;

(c) Whether the parties' relationship becomes spousal within the definition set out in the *Family Law Act*;

(d) Any direct contribution by a party to the preservation, maintenance, improvement, operation, or management of the other party's assets;

(e) The degree to which the parties do or do not rely on the terms of the agreement during the relationship;

(f) A party's contribution of some or all of that party's assets to a trust in which that party is a beneficiary, has a vested interest not subject to divestment, has the power to transfer some or all of the trust property to that party, or that party has the power to terminate the trust and have the property revert to that party; or

(g) The existence of family property or family debt located outside of British Columbia that cannot be practically divided.

7. CB and Dick are entering into this Agreement to:

(a) Confirm ownership, management, and division of property;

(i) If their relationship becomes spousal;

(ii) In the event their relationship ends either before or after it becomes spousal;

(iii) If one of them predeceases the other during the relationship.

(b) Determine spousal support obligations if their relationship ends;

(c) Permit each of them to engage in plans for their personal future and estate planning as they wish;

(d) Achieve certainty; and,

(e) Avoid acrimony and litigation if their relationship ends.

8. In negotiating this Agreement, the parties have considered and have agreed that it should continue to apply if there is any change of circumstance affecting a party's health, financial independence, or future prospects, including, without limiting the generality of the foregoing, the following issues or categories of issues:

(a) a party becoming unemployed or otherwise ceasing to be financially self-supporting,

(b) a party suffering continuing ill health or a short-term or long-term disability,

(c) a party subordinating career or economic prospects to the career or economic prospects of the other,

(d) unequal distribution of the family expenses between the parties,

(e) a party providing care, assistance, or financial support to the other party,

(f) a relative of a party living with the parties, or otherwise requiring care, assistance, or financial support,

(g) changes in the value of a party's assets as a result of changes in the economy, and

(h) either party receiving an inheritance, using or declining to use an inheritance for the benefit of the other party.

EFFECTIVE DATE

9. This Agreement takes effect when the last of the parties to the agreement signs it and a reference to "the signing of this Agreement" means the date the last of the parties to the agreement signed it.

10. This Agreement is binding upon CB and Dick:

(a) During their relationship prior to marriage, whether or not it qualifies as spousal under the *Family Law Act*;

(b) During their marriage, if they marry; and,

(c) After their relationship, if it ends.

DEFINITION OF "SEPARATION"

11. For the purposes of this Agreement, the parties' relationship will be deemed to have ended and a separation to have occurred on the first of the following events to occur:

(a) voluntary termination of their cohabitation as a result of a breakdown in the relationship by either party or both of them;

(b) by written notice delivered by one party to the other that their relationship is terminated, whether or not they are living in separate residences at the time written notice is delivered;

(c) the date declared by a court of competent jurisdiction as the date of the parties' separation (all of which are defined as a "Separation" herein).

LIVING EXPENSES

12. Each party will be self-supporting during their cohabitation and, if they marry, their marriage.

13. Each party will contribute substantially equal amounts toward the cost of their joint household while residing together,

a) including but not restricted to paying for repairs, insurance, mortgage payments, property tax, utilities, and the like,

b) however, the parties recognize that if one party makes contributions which are not offset by the benefits he or she receives, said benefits shall be considered to be a gift from the contributing party and do not establish a pattern of dependency, obligation to pay support, or a form of unjust enrichment and resulting deprivation either now in the future.

NO SPOUSAL SUPPORT IN THE EVENT OF SEPARATION

14. In the event of a Separation notwithstanding any change of circumstances no matter how unforeseen or radical,

(a) Neither party shall claim from the other interim or permanent spousal support (whether contractual, compensatory, or non-compensatory), or other form of compensation from the other based on actual or perceived economic prejudice suffered by reason of the relationship;

(b) Each party forever discharges and releases the other party from all such claims;

(c) Each party specifically waives and renounces any claims or right to claim that he or she may now or hereafter have for spousal support, maintenance, or alimony for himself or herself from the other party, and shall be precluded and estopped from ever bringing any action or proceeding for interim or permanent spousal support or support for himself or herself from the other party pursuant to the *Family Law Act*, the *Divorce Act,* or any other statute or law.

PROPERTY

15. Except as otherwise provided in this Agreement,

(a) all property, including the Pets,[107] acquired by CB before the date of this Agreement and set out in Schedule "D" is CB's "separate property" and will remain so after the relationship ends.

(b) all property acquired by Dick before the date of this Agreement and set out in Schedule "E" is Dick's "separate property" and will remain so after the relationship ends.

16. The property referred to in the previous paragraph and all "separate property" includes:

(a) any income produced by the property,

(b) any growth or increase in value of the property, and

(c) any property acquired in exchange for the property or with

(i) the proceeds from sale of the property or its substitute, or

(ii) the income produced by the property.

17. Either party may acquire or dispose of separate property without the consent of the other.

18. Any property solely acquired by a party during the relationship together with any growth or increase in that property is the separate property of the party who solely acquired it, unless

(a) it is registered in both parties' names, or

(b) the parties record in writing that it is co-owned.

19. Unless the parties otherwise agree in writing, ownership of co-owned assets will be in the same proportion as the contribution made by each party to the purchase. For the purposes of this paragraph, "contribution" means a direct financial contribution and does not include value for labour unless otherwise agreed in writing.

20. In the event of a Separation, save and except for the purposes of enforcing this Agreement, neither party will claim an interest in, or a right to compensation with respect to, the property of the other pursuant to this Agreement and, without limiting the generality of the foregoing, neither will make such a claim based on:

(a) the law pertaining to trusts or unjust enrichment;

(b) the *Family Law Act* or similar legislation, whether or not the property was used for a family purpose, or

(c) any direct or indirection contribution to property owned by the other, whether or not savings occurred through effective management of the household or otherwise.

GIFTS AND WINDFALLS

21. All inheritances, windfalls, gifts, or damages for personal injury received by either party during the relationship or after it ends, or any growth in invested inheritances, windfalls, gifts, or damages due to personal injury, are the separate property of the recipient.

22. With respect to gifts:

(a) Nothing in this Agreement prevents either party from making gifts to the other;

(b) Except as otherwise provided in this Agreement, if property is purchased by one party and placed in the name of the other or in both names as co-owners, the transaction is not a gift and, in the event of a separation, must be divided on the basis of the financial contributions of both parties;

(c) A gift received by one party or the other becomes the recipient's separate property;

(d) Unless a third party specifically provides to the contrary, a gift from the third party is the recipient's separate property.

(e) A gift from a third party that is used as a down payment for the purchase of land or a residence

(i) is traceable into the purchased property and any substitute for it, and

(ii) remains the separate property of the recipient.

CB's REAL PROPERTY (aka the "House")

23. The House is the separate property of CB, subject to the following paragraphs, and shall remain registered in her name alone.

24. It shall be solely within CB's discretion whether or not to list the House for sale at any time, and should she decide to list the House for sale, she shall have sole conduct of sale.

25. CB will be responsible for the mortgage, property taxes, utilities, and all expenses required to maintain the House.

26. Any and all rental income from the House shall be CB's separate property.

27. While the parties reside together at the House,

a) Dick will pay at least one half (50%) of all major expenses toward maintaining the House, including but not limited to mortgage, repairs, insurance, taxes, and renovations,

b) If Dick voluntarily contributes an additional amount without an agreement in writing regarding that additional amount, such additional amount contributed by Dick is a gift to CB, and

c) Both parties are responsible for maintaining a record of their financial contributions, such as banking records, for the purposes of this section and section 29.

28. Whether or not the parties become spouses as defined in the *Family Law Act*, in the event of a Separation, Dick:

(a) must vacate the House within 60 days;

(b) shall not pledge or use as collateral for a liability his entitlement to be paid in accordance with the above sub-paragraph in any manner that would result in an encumbrance being placed on title to the House;

(c) shall not have the ability or right to compel CB to sell the House.

29. In the event of a Separation, and within 120 days of Dick vacating the House;

a) If Dick has strictly complied with section 27, i.e., has contributed substantially 50% of the finances required to maintain, and/or improve, the House, including mortgage, repairs, renovations, property taxes, insurance, etc., CB shall pay to Dick one-half of the net lift in value of the House at the date of Separation;

b) If Dick has not complied with section 27, then Dick's share of the net lift will be commensurate with his financial contributions such that both parties see the same return on their respective investments in the House, calculated as per Schedule "E,"[108] unless,

c) Dick's contributions have been an average of $1,000[109] or less per month during the relationship, in which case he shall receive 0% of the value of the House.

30. If the parties cannot agree on the fair market value of the House at the date of the Separation, they shall each pay 50% of the cost of an appraisal by a certified appraiser ("the Joint Appraiser") to determine the fair market value of the House. If either party disagrees with the Joint Appraiser's determination of the fair market value, he or she can obtain a second appraisal at his or her own cost and the fair market value shall be the average of the Joint Appraiser's determination and the second appraiser's determination.

DICK'S REAL PROPERTY (aka the "Condo")

31. The Condo is the separate property of Dick and shall remain registered in his name alone.

32. Dick will be responsible for the mortgage, property taxes, utilities, and all expenses required to maintain the Condo.

33. Any and all rental income from the Condo shall be Dick's separate property.

34. Any capital gains tax resulting from a disposition of the Condo by Dick shall be Dick's sole responsibility, without contribution by CB.

DEBTS

35. CB is solely responsible for paying CB's Debts.

36. Dick is solely responsible for paying Dick's Debts.

37. Neither party will, without the written consent of the other party, use funds from joint savings, should the parties create joint accounts in the future, to pay personal debts.

38. Neither party will be responsible for any future debt or liability of the other, unless the debt is a debt incurred in accordance with paragraph 41 below.

39. A party will reimburse the other party for any expense or loss the other party incurs with respect to the first party's current or future debts and liabilities.

40. Except as specifically provided herein, either party may incur liabilities and pledge that party's separate property as security for those liabilities without the consent of the other.

41. Each party is responsible for half of any debt or liability incurred:

(a) jointly, or

(b) by one party with the other party's written consent.

42. Neither party shall:

(a) pledge the credit of the other;

(b) bind the other for debt as agents; or

(c) fail to pay or discharge past debts for which that party is responsible.

43. A party in breach of sub-clauses (a) through (c) in the previous paragraph above shall save harmless and indemnify the other with respect to any liability arising out of the breach.

PENSIONS

44. Any new pensions acquired by either party during the relationship will not be divided pursuant to Part 6 of the *Family Law Act* nor successor legislation nor applicable federal legislation, unless,

a) Both parties contribute to pension or equivalent

retirement savings plans during the course of their relationship;

b) Material change in circumstance requires a revision of section 46. For further clarity, material change in circumstance would include, but not be limited to

i) illness preventing pensionable employment

ii) mutual decision, recorded in writing, that one party cease pensionable employment.

CB'S PENSION (s)

45. Any pension property or payments made to CB from CB's Pension (s) shall be CB's separate property.

46. While their relationship continues, CB is not required to maintain Dick as the beneficiary of any survivor benefits of CB's Pension that CB has or acquires during the relationship or marriage, or to make any designation in her will that would result in Dick receiving funds related to CB's Pension. However, if after the date on which this Agreement takes effect, CB takes steps by will or otherwise that result in Dick receiving funds relating to CB's Pension upon her death while the relationship continues, such funds are a gift to Dick.

47. In the event of a Separation, CB shall retain as her separate property:

(a) All interest in, entitlement to, and contributions made by and on behalf of CB and benefits accruing to her in CB's Pension (s), if any, and

(b) Any benefits payable to her prior to CB's Pension (s) maturing and when CB's Pension (s) matures.

48. In the event of Separation, Dick:

(a) waives, releases, and gives up forever the right to apply for a share in CB's Pension, the right to receive funds relating to CB's Pension, or other benefits of CB under CB's Pension;

(b) will do everything reasonably necessary to assist in making the foregoing sub-paragraph fully effective, including but not limited to completing all necessary documents and forms as are required to ensure the foregoing paragraph is fully effective, including Form P7, P5;

(c) In the event any payment is made to Dick after Separation in relation to CB's Pension as a result of an unchanged beneficiary designation or unchanged will, Dick shall hold any such payment in trust for CB's estate and shall owe CB's estate all the duties of a trustee in relation to such payment.

49. In the event that CB transfers CB's Pension to a locked-in RRSP outside the pension plan (the "New RRSP"), the New RRSP, together with any growth in the value of the New RRSP and any income or withdrawals from it shall be CB's separate property.

50. CB is not required to maintain Dick as the beneficiary of the New RRSP, or to make any designation in her will that would result in Dick receiving funds related to the New RRSP. However, if after the date on which this Agreement takes effect, CB takes steps by will or otherwise that result in Dick receiving funds relating to the New RRSP upon her death while the relationship continues, such funds are a gift to Dick.

51. In the event of Separation, Dick:

(a) waives, releases, and gives up forever any right to the New RRSP;

(b) will do everything reasonably necessary to assist in making the foregoing sub-paragraph fully effective, including but not limited to completing all necessary documents and forms as are required to ensure the foregoing paragraph is fully effective;

(c) In the event any payment is made to Dick after Separation in relation to the New RRSP as a result of an unchanged beneficiary designation or unchanged will, Dick shall hold any such payment in trust for CB's estate and shall owe CB's estate all the duties of a trustee in relation to such payment.

DICK'S PENSION (s)

[About 5 paragraphs basically repeating the above, waiving claim on Dick's pensions]

CANADA PENSION PLAN

56. While their relationship or marriage continues, Dick and CB's interests in any pre-retirement or post-retirement survivor benefits under the Canada Pension Plan will be determined under the *Canada Pension Plan*, RSC 1985, c. C-8, or successor act thereto ("the Canada Pension Plan").

57. In the event of a Separation:

    (a) Dick and CB's unadjusted pensionable earnings under the Canada Pension Plan will not be equalized under sections 55, 55.1, and 55.2 of its governing Act, and

    (b) Neither party will apply for equalization of the other party's respective unadjusted pensionable earnings pursuant to the Canada Pension Plan.

WILLS

58. Unless otherwise provided for in a will made after the date of this Agreement, on the death of a party, the surviving party will not:

    (a) Share in any testate or intestate benefit from the estate, or

    (b) Act as personal representative of the deceased party and the estate of the deceased party will be distributed as if the surviving party had died first.

59. A party is free to make a will leaving that party's separate property to such beneficiaries as that party may independently choose.

LIFE INSURANCE

60. It is in CB's sole discretion to make or change any available beneficiary designations to any person she wishes in relation to any life insurance policy in her name.

61. It is in Dick's sole discretion to make or change any available beneficiary designations to any person he wishes in relation to any life insurance policy in his name.

GENERAL

62. If either party seeks a divorce or takes any proceedings with respect to the parties' assets or responsibilities to each other, this Agreement shall:

(a) be filed or exhibited in such proceedings and the Divorce Order or final order in the event the parties do not marry shall contain a consent dismissal of all claims by one party against the other except for the purposes of enforcing this Agreement;

(b) continue in effect after any Order is made in the proceedings; and

(c) survive a divorce.

63. This Agreement shall be amended only by a written Agreement executed in the same manner as this Agreement.

64. If a dispute arises concerning this Agreement, it shall be governed by the laws of the Province of British Columbia.

65. This Agreement shall enure to the benefit of and be binding upon the parties and their respective heirs, executors, administrators, and assigns.

66. The parties shall execute and deliver such further documents and do such things as may reasonably be required to carry out and give full effect to this Agreement.

67. Each party shall be responsible for the fees of his or her solicitor with respect to the negotiation, preparation, and carrying into effect of this Agreement.

68. This Agreement constitutes the entire Agreement between the parties and there are no representations, promises, warranties, covenants, or conditions other than those expressly set forth in this Agreement.

RELEASES

69. (a) This Agreement is a full and final settlement of all issues between the parties and all rights and obligations arising out of their spousal or marital relationship;

(b) Each party hereby forever discharges and releases the other from all claims at law, in equity or by statute including, without restricting the generality of the foregoing, the *Family Law Act*, the *Wills Variation Act*, the *Estate Administration Act*, and the *Divorce Act*, and amending Acts thereto with respect to:

(i) maintenance;

(ii) property;

(iii) succession rights; and

(iv) any other matter arising from the spousal or marital relationship.

NO SETTING ASIDE OR VARIATION OF AGREEMENT

70. The parties are aware that the law provides for judicial intervention in this Agreement in prescribed circumstances.

71. The parties wish to make it clear that it is their intention that:

(a) Each of them rely on this Agreement to be enforced according to its terms;

(b) Neither of them would have entered into the Agreement if he or she believed that the other would apply at any time to vary it or set it aside.

72. The parties acknowledge that each of them is prepared to abide by the terms of this Agreement because each recognizes that:

(a) The importance to each of them of being able to rely on it far outweighs the risk that it may operate unfairly at some future date;

(b) The impossibility of returning the parties to the positions they occupied before they entered this Agreement would make any variation or setting aside, however fair viewed solely in the changed circumstances, unfair on the whole because all dealings with their property after the date of this Agreement will have been based on the binding nature of this Agreement.

73. Each party expressly waives the protection of section 93 and section 164 of the *Family Law Act*, successor legislation, or similar legislation in any other jurisdiction where they may happen to reside.

PARTICULARS OF EXECUTION

74. Dick and CB separately acknowledge that:

(a) his or her present and future needs have been adequately provided for by this Agreement;

(b) all matters in dispute between them including those

pertaining to family assets and to real and personal property interests have been settled to his or her satisfaction;

(c) he or she has received independent legal advice and has been advised as to his or her rights against and obligations to the other;

(d) he or she has made full disclosure to the other of his or her financial position;

(e) if either party makes or pursues a claim against the other, this Agreement shall be pled as full estoppel and defence to any such claim and shall further form the basis of a consent order in those proceedings so as to maintain the full force and effect of this Agreement; and

(f) he or she has read the entire Agreement carefully, knows and understands its contents, and has executed it voluntarily without any undue influence or coercion by the other (this last bit was part of the original cohab I had with Dick, and its irony is untended.

END NOTES & BIBLIOGRAPHY

[1] W. Bradford Wilcox "The Evolution of Divorce," *National Affairs*, no. 53 (Winter 2023). https://www.nationalaffairs.com/publications/detail/the-evolution-of-divorce.

[2] Julien D. Payne, "Family Law in Canada: Past, Present and Future" (presentation, Ottawa Chapter of the Ontario Association for Family Mediation, Ottawa, ON, June 6, 2013).

[3] Family Law page for the Government of Canada can be found here: https://www.justice.gc.ca/eng/fl-df/index.html with links to additional information.

[4] The thirteen lawyers I consulted over the course of my relationship with Dick and our breakup are referred to in the order in which I consulted them.

[5] Percentages from Statistics Canada, release date: July 13, 2022: https://www150.statcan.gc.ca/t1/tbl1/en/tv.action?pid=9810012501

[6] *Three Brains, How the heart, brain, and gut influence mental health and identity*, Karen Jensen, Mind Publishing, 2016

[7] *The Gut-Brain Connection*, online, The Cleveland Clinic, https://my.clevelandclinic.org/health/body/the-gut-brain-connection

[8] *Don't Trust Your Gut*, Eric Bonabeau, Harvard Business Review, May 2003, https://hbr.org/2003/05/dont-trust-your-gut

[9] "*Family Law: Historical Background*," jrank.org. https://law.jrank.org/pages/6744/Family-Law-Historical-Background.html#ixzz7Myr8Tt2d

[10] *Common law: Defining what it is and what you need to know*, online, Thomson Reuters, Nov 15, 2022 https://legal.thomsonreuters.com/en/insights/articles/what-is-common-law

[11] *Canon law*, online, Cornell Law School, Jun 2021, https://www.law.cornell.edu/wex/canon_law

[12] Hamilton, Vivian E., "Principles of U.S. Family Law" (2006). *Faculty Publications*. 184, https://scholarship.law.wm.edu/facpubs/184

[13] Christina, Common Ego: https://www.commonego.com https://www.youtube.com/@CommonEgo

[14] https://doctor-ramani.com/; https://survivingnarcissism.tv/about-surviving-narcissism/about-dr-les-carter/; and https://www.stephanielynlifecoaching.com/.

[15] *Healthy vs Unhealthy Boundaries*, Eleanor Beeslaar, online, April, 2019 https://healthyrelationshipsinitiative.org/healthy-vs-unhealthy-boundaries/

[16] Some recommended reading: Harriet Lerner (*The Dance of Anger: A Woman's Guide to Changing the Patterns of Intimate Relationships*, William Morrow, 2014); Ramani Durvasula (*Don't You Know Who I Am? How to Stay Sane in an Era of Narcissism, Entitlement, and Incivility*, Post Hill Press, 2019); Les Carter (*When Pleasing You is Killing Me*, BookBaby, 2018, https://www.youtube.com/c/SurvivingNarcissism).

[17] According to Dr. Joan Mundin, quoted in this article: https://psychcentral.com/relationships/love-versus-infatuation#infatuation-in-a-relationship.

[18] According to John Gottman, the four horsemen of the end of a relationship are criticism, contempt, defensiveness, and stonewalling (https://www.gottman.com/blog/the-four-horsemen-recognizing-criticism-contempt-defensiveness-and-stonewalling/). I think there's a fifth horseman: social media, which can engender narcissism, unrealistic expectations, and anxiety.

[19] Lee-Young, J, Vancouver Sun, online, April 19, 2022, https://vancouversun.com/news/local-news/vancouver-third-least-affordable-city-demographia

[20] Matthew Hussey, http://www.matthewhussey.com/ and https://www.youtube.com/@thematthewhussey

[21] *The Aesop for Children*, presented by The Library of Congress, https://read.gov/aesop/index.html

[22] Millon, T. et al, *Personality Disorders in Modern Life*, 2004, John Wiley & Sons, Inc.

[23] *Diagnostic and Statistical Manual of Mental Disorders*, American Psychiatric Association, https://www.psychiatry.org/psychiatrists/practice/dsm

[24] Kaurin A, Beeney JE, Stepp SD, Scott LN, Woods WC, Pilkonis PA, Wright AGC. *Attachment and Borderline Personality Disorder: Differential Effects on Situational Socio-Affective Processes*. Affect Sci. 2020 Sep;1(3):117-127. doi: 10.1007/s42761-020-00017-7. Epub 2020 Sep 18. PMID: 33718882; PMCID: PMC7954219.

[25] *Long-term Effects of Traumatic Brain Injury*, online, Dec 6, 2021, University of Utah, https://healthcare.utah.edu/healthfeed/postings/2021/12/traumatic-brain-injury-effects.

[26] Lyvers et al., "Risky Cannabis Use is Associated with Alexithymia, Frontal Lobe Dysfunction, and Impulsivity in Young Adult Cannabis Users," *Journal of Psychoactive Drugs* 45, no. 5 (2013): 394-403. https://www.tandfonline.com/doi/full/10.1080/02791072.2013.844525

[27] *Is Marijuana Safe and Effective as Medicine?*, National Institute on

Drug Abuse, April 13, 2021. https://nida.nih.gov/publications/research-reports/marijuana/marijuana-safe-effective-medicine.

[28] Riley, Dan, *The Peter Pan Syndrome: Men Who Have Never Grown Up* (New York: Dodd Mead, 1983).

[29] Yakely, Jessica, *Current understanding of narcissism and narcissistic personality disorder* (Cambridge University Press, July, 2018) https://www.cambridge.org/core/journals/bjpsych-advances/article/current-understanding-of-narcissism-and-narcissistic-personality-disorder/4AA8B04FB352F8E00AA7988B63EBE973.

[30] *What is Love Bombing*, online, February 2023, Cleveland Clinic, with psychologist Alaina Tiani, https://health.clevelandclinic.org/love-bombing/

[31] Murray, Megan, "Older Men Dating Younger Women: What Online Dating Data Tells U"s, *The Date Mix* (online), May 2021. www.zoosk.com/date-mix/dating-advice/older-men-dating-younger-women/

[32] Bruch, Elizabeth E. Bruch, Newman, M.E.J., "Aspirational Pursuit of Mates in Online Dating Markets," *Journal of Science Advances* 4, no. 8 (2018). https://www.science.org/doi/10.1126/sciadv.aap9815

[33] Vaknin, Sam, "The Narcissist as Eternal Child," *HealthyPlace* online, January 5, 2008. https://www.healthyplace.com/personality-disorders/malignant-self-love/the-narcissist-as-eternal-child.

[34] Georgia Kiziridou, trans. by S. Poimenidou, "Wendy's Syndrome: When the Partner Becomes the Nanny," *Animartists International* online, May 25, 2018. https://en.animartists.com/2018/05/25/wendys-syndrome-when-the-partner-becomes-the-nanny/.

[35] Caveat - I love my mom. She's a strong, independent, intelligent woman who suffered terribly in her youth and loved us the best she could.

[36] Williams, R, *All About Stonewalling and Gaslighting*, https://psychcentral.com/health/stonewalling-and-gaslighting

[37] Lisitsa, E, for The Gottman Institute https://www.gottman.com/blog/the-four-horsemen-recognizing-criticism-contempt-defensiveness-and-stonewalling/.

[38] Lerner, H, *The Dance of Anger*, William Morrow Paperbacks, 2014)

[39] Brené Brown on boundaries https://www.youtube.com/watch?v=TLOoa8UGqxA

[40] https://brenebrown.com/resources/dare-to-lead-list-of-values/

[41] . See Dan Riley's *The Peter Pan Syndrome* and articles like this one: https://www.medicalnewstoday.com/articles/peter-pan-syndrome#causes.

[42] https://www.psychologytoday.com/ca/blog/meet-catch-and-keep/202002/is-the-7-year-itch-myth-or-reality

[43] Les Carter, "How Narcissists Gaslight Themselves Before They Gaslight You," YouTube, 12:56 min., April 4, 2022. https://www.youtube.com/watch?v=vBZ7woWOHbs.

[44] Zoppi, L., *Trauma Bonding Explained*, Medical News Today, April, 2023, https://www.medicalnewstoday.com/articles/trauma-bonding

[45] Carnes, Patrick, *The Betrayal Bond: Breaking Free of Exploitative Relationships* (Health Communications Inc, 1997, rev 2019)

[46] John Tholen, author of *Focused Positivity*, quoted in *Forbes Magazine* in 2022: https://www.forbes.com/health/mind/what-is-trauma-bonding/.

[47] C. Raypole, T. Rush, *How to Recognize and Break Trama Bonds*, Healthline, June 2023, https://www.healthline.com/health/mental-health/trauma-bonding

[48] Hower, R, *The Definition of Insanity – Perseverance versus perseveration*, July, 2009, https://www.psychologytoday.com/intl/blog/in-therapy/200907/the-definition-insanity

[49] On Family Law in Canada - https://www.justice.gc.ca/eng/fl-df/

[50] From Legal Aid BC: https://family.legalaid.bc.ca/common-questions/my-new-spouse-responsible-paying-child-support-my-children-previous-relationship.

[51] Department of Justice Canada, *The Federal Child Support Guidelines: Step-by-Step*, justice.gc.ca, December 21, 2022. https://www.justice.gc.ca/eng/rp-pr/fl-lf/child-enfant/guide/toc-tdm.html.

[52] Williams, G., "Child Support Laws and Expectations: The most important thing to remember about child support law is that it's designed to help your child," *U.S. News—World Report*, May 2019.

[53] Khazan, Olga, "Nearly Half of All Murdered Women Are Killed by Romantic Partners," *The Atlantic*, July 2017. https://www.theatlantic.com/health/archive/2017/07/homicides-women/534306/.

[54] If you are a victim of domestic abuse, there is little in family law, let alone any kind of agreement, that can protect you. Please seek help as soon as you can. Get out as soon as you *safely* can. And with all my heart I wish you safekeeping and Godspeed.

[55] Meuller, W. Morgan, D., "Contracts," *Thomson Reuters Westlaw Canada* online. https://www.westlawcanada.com/academic/.

[56] Ibid.

[57] Yousefi, L., *How to Adjourn Your BC Family Law Trial or Hearings*, for YLAW Group, June 2017, https://www.ylaw.ca/blog/how-adjourn-your-bc-family-law-trial/

[58] O.J. Simpson Trial, Britannica, https://www.britannica.com/event/O-J-Simpson-trial

[59] Online Help Guide – Supreme Court of BC: https://supremecourtbc.ca/family-law/before-trial/discovery/examinations-discovery

[60] *Let it Go*, Idina Menzel, https://www.youtube.com/watch?v=moSFlvxnbgk

[61] I had a federal pension, subject to Canada's Pension Division Act: https://laws-lois.justice.gc.ca/eng/acts/P-6.7/page-1.html#h-414227.

[62] Department of Justice Canada, *The Divorce Act Changes Explained*, justice.gc.ca, February 23, 2022. www.justice.gc.ca/eng/fl-df/cfl-mdf/dace-clde/index.html.

[63] Honest, I'm not: my ex-husband was a good man, my current significant other is a lovely man, my father was a great man, I have lots of friends who are lovely men, but stats are stats.

[64] Breiding, Mathew L., et al., *Intimate Partner Violence Surveillance: Uniform Definitions and Recommended Data Elements, Version 2.0*, Atlanta, GA: National Center for Injury Prevention and Control, Centers for Disease Control and Prevention, 2015. https://www.cdc.gov/violenceprevention/intimatepartnerviolence/fastfact.html.

[65] Blind to the point of exposing children to domestic violence. Mia Rabson, "Keira's Law, Requiring Judicial Training on Domestic Violence, Passes Second Stage in House, *Globe and Mail*, April 29, 2022. https://www.theglobeandmail.com/politics/article-keiras-law-requiring-judicial-training-on-domestic-violence-passes/.

[66] Recommended reading before you write your cohab: *Marriage, a History: How Love Conquered Marriage* by sociologist Stephanie Coontz (New York: Penguin Books, 2006).

[67] See *Hemingway v. Scott*, Court of Appeals of Indiana, Opinion 39A04-1604-PL-957 2017.

[68] *The 5 'Blue Zones" where the world's healthiest people live*, National Geographic, Sept, 2023 https://www.nationalgeographic.com/premium/article/5-blue-zones-where-the-worlds-healthiest-people-live Also, https://www.bluezones.com.

[69] Weisman, Mary-Lou, "The History of Retirement, from Early Man to AARP," *New York Times* online, March 21, 1999. https://www.nytimes.com/1999/03/21/jobs/the-history-of-retirement-from-early-man-to-aarp.html.

[70] Lake, R. *How to Protect Your pension in Divorce: 4 Ways*, for Investopedia, April, 2023 https://www.investopedia.com/articles/retirement/072916/how-protect-your-pension-divorce.asp

[71] Types of pension plans, Aug 6, 2021, https://www.canadalife.com/investing-saving/retirement/pension-plans/types-of-pension-plans.html

[72] Separation or divorce and your pension, https://pspp.pensionsbc.ca/dividing-your-pension

[73] Balbi, Lonny L., "Steps to Using the Spousal Support Advisory Guidelines," justice.gc.ca, October, 2009. https://www.justice.gc.ca/eng/fl-df/spousal-epoux/topic-theme/dir/wo-sans.html

[74] Spousal Support Advisory Guidelines, https://www.justice.gc.ca/eng/rp-pr/fl-lf/spousal-epoux/spag/index.html

[75] A resource on this topic is the blog by BC's YLaw group. For example, see "How to Terminate Spousal Support or Alimony in BC" by Leena Yousefi, May 2018, at https://www.ylaw.ca/blog/how-terminate-spousal-support-alimony-bc/.

[76] Scott, Shelby B. et al., *Reasons for Divorce and Recollections of Premarital Intervention: Implications for Improving Relationship Education*, Couple and Family Psychology 2, no. 2 (2013):131–145. https://doi.org/10.1037/a0032025.

[77] *Thomson v. Young*, 2014 BCSC 799, [61]. https://www.bccourts.ca/jdb-txt/SC/14/07/2014BCSC0799.htm.

[78] Section 85 of BC's *FLA* describes what is excluded property here: https://www.bclaws.gov.bc.ca/civix/document/id/complete/statreg/11025_05#section85.

[79] For example, here's Ontario: https://www.ontario.ca/laws/statute/90f03.

[80] Feldstein Family Law Group (Ontario) (https://www.separation.ca/help-centre/division-of-property/inheritances-gifts/) and Candid Legal Law Corporation (BC) (https://www.candidlegal.com/post/share-inheritance-in-divorce).

[81] A good resource for summarizing BC's *FLA* is John-Paul Boyd, "Basic Principles of Property and Debt in Family Law," *JP Boyd on Family Law* (a Clicklaw Wikibook), 2019. The page on property and debt division is referenced here: https://wiki.clicklaw.bc.ca/index.php?title=Basic_Principles_of_Property_and_Debt_in_Family_Law.

[82] Skrypnek, Jane, "Dog ownership split between multiple exes makes for tricky B.C. custody case B.C. woman ordered to return dog to ex, ex's old partner despite claim it was gifted to her verbally", *The Northern View*, May 25, 2022 https://www.thenorthernview.com/news/dog-ownership-split-between-multiple-exes-makes-for-tricky-b-c-custody-case/.

[83] Anderson, Patrick, "Bill seeks to give pets a voice in R.I. divorce cases + Poll", *The Providence Journal*, February 28, 2017 https://www.providencejournal.com/story/news/2017/02/28/bill-seeks-to-give-pets-voice-in-ri-divorce-cases-poll/22049801007/

[84] The Canadian Press, "B.C. plans family law changes to decide who gets the pets when couples split", *The Times Colonist*, March 27, 2023 https://www.timescolonist.com/local-news/bc-plans-family-law-changes-to-decide-who-gets-the-pets-when-couples-split-6767787

[85] BC Laws, https://www.bclaws.gov.bc.ca/civix/document/id/complete/statreg/11025_10.

[86] In BC's Supreme Court, it's more than 97%! https://supremecourtbc.ca/civil-law/overview/before-you-sue

[87] The original cohab stipulated valuation at separation, not at time of division, which is contrary to BC's FLA, which states that it's the date of agreement or trial that is used for valuation. But not all jurisdictions may be the same. According to an article about Ontario's FLA: https://www.separation.ca/help-center/division-of-property/calculating-division-of-property/ valuation date can become contentious.

[88] Maclean Family Law, https://macleanfamilylaw.ca/2017/04/24/vancouver-family-law-settlement-lawyers/

[89] Liang, Lauren, July, 2011, for Clark Wilson, https://www.cwilson.com/supreme-court-of-canada-clarifies-unjust-enrichment-principles/.

[90] https://www.cwilson.com/a-refresher-on-resulting-and-constructive-trusts/.

[91] *Linde v. Linde*, 2019, BCSC 1586, https://www.canlii.org/en/bc/bcsc/doc/2019/2019bcsc1586/2019bcsc1586.html?autocompleteStr=linde%20v%20linde&autocompletePos=8.

[92] Thomson Reuters, *Practical Law*, https://ca.practicallaw.thomsonreuters.com/1-518-6318?transitionType=Default&contextData=(sc.Default)&firstPage=true.

[93] https://macleanfamilylaw.ca/2019/06/15/vancouver-oral-family-agreements/

[94] Mueller, W., Morgan, D. "Contracts," Thomson Reuters Westlaw Canada online. https://www.westlawcanada.com/academic/. Italics are mine.

[95] Berthin v Berthin, 2016, BCCA 104, https://www.bccourts.ca/jdb-txt/ca/16/01/2016BCCA0104cor1.htm.

[96] https://canliiconnects.org/en/summaries/33998.

[97] For cases in Canada, see https://www.canlii.org/en/. In the US, it depends on the state you live in. This site is a start: https://law.justia.com/cases/. Cornell U runs a Legal Information Institute: https://www.law.cornell.edu/wex/family_court

[98] https://www.bccourts.ca/supreme_court/.

[99] https://www.ontariocourts.ca/scj/practice/practice-directions/list/.

[100] https://www.bccourts.ca/jdb-txt/sc/18/15/2018BCSC1533.htm.

[101] https://www.bccourts.ca/jdb-txt/sc/16/13/2016BCSC1337.htm.

[102] Voss, Christopher, *Never Split the Difference: Negotiating as If Your Life Depended on It*, Harper Business, May 17 2016.

[103] Sadly, Ms. Ford died, far too young, in 2013, but not before she helped many people through the pain of divorce and the rebirth that can come with it. http://thefordinstitute.com/.

[104] Judicial case conference: an attempt to air the case before a judge. I suspect this was a strategy to spook me into settling, by forcing me to listen to

a judge about how much more I'll lose if I don't settle under the flawed CA. But I have no proof of this.

[105] Schedules are like appendices, with technical details such as asset valuations and previous agreements that may affect this one, but the information in them is so specific that I don't include them here.

[106] *Recitals* is a legal term for the alphabetized items listed above.

[107] As I mentioned in Chapter 7: "Other Chops of Lamb," furry family members are considered "property." Distasteful, in my view, but that's the current state of the law.

[108] This was part of the much-contended amended agreement, which basically included a model in which both of us would see the same rate of return on our investment in my house, which seemed fair to me, but I couldn't get Dick to execute it, for some unfathomable reason.

[109] A somewhat arbitrary number, roughly 25% of what it would cost to rent a place like the House in Vancouver at the time of this writing. According to my boundaries, if someone would prefer not to contribute in a significant way, then it may make sense to charge them a nominal rent. But if they're renting, should they still get a cut of the increase in value of the property? I don't think so, but you may feel differently.

[110] This last bit was included in the original cohab agreement, and its irony unintended.

ACKNOWLEDGEMENTS

I would like to thank all the people who tirelessly listened to her complaints about her ex before she finally gave up on the relationship, especially my family and my loved ones. I'm grateful they are still in my life after all of that.

I would like to thank the friend who read the book twice and provided editing, for the price of a bottle of Pinot no less

I would like to acknowledge the editors who made this book better, and all the lawyers I consulted with. I learned a lot from each and every one of you.

ABOUT THE AUTHOR

Cinoma Bronhill

Writing under a pen name, the author works as an environmental engineer, developing protection meausures for endangered species. When she's not trying to save things or writing stuff, you can find her on a bike or on her horse

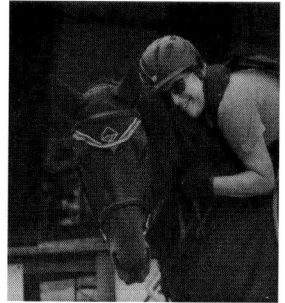

Manufactured by Amazon.ca
Acheson, AB